A Guide to Psychological Debriefing

of related interest

A Bolt from the Blue
Coping with Disasters and Acute Traumas
Salli Saari
Translated by Annira Silver
ISBN 978 1 84310 313 4

The Madness of Our Lives
Experiences of Mental Breakdown and Recovery
Penny Gray
Foreword by Peter Campbell
ISBN 978 1 84310 057 7

Living Alongside a Child's Recovery
Therapeutic Parenting with Traumatized Children
Billy Pughe and Terry Philpot
Foreword by Mary Walsh, co-founder and Chief Executive of SACCS
ISBN 978 1 84310 328 8

Reaching the Vulnerable Child
Therapy with Traumatized Children
Janie Rymaszewska and Terry Philpot
Foreword by Mary Walsh, co-founder and Chief Executive of SACCS
ISBN 978 1 84310 329 5

The Child's Own Story
Life Story Work with Traumatized Children
Richard Rose and Terry Philpot
Foreword by Mary Walsh, co-founder and Chief Executive of SACCS
ISBN 978 1 84310 287 8

Expressive and Creative Arts Methods for Trauma Survivors
Edited by Lois Carey
ISBN 978 1 84310 386 8

Counselling Adult Survivors of Child Sexual Abuse
3rd edition
Christiane Sanderson
ISBN 9781843103356

Counselling and Psychotherapy with Refugees
Dick Blackwell
ISBN 978 1 84310 316 5

A Guide to Psychological Debriefing

Managing Emotional Decompression and Post-Traumatic Stress Disorder

David Kinchin

Foreword by Gordon Turnbull

Jessica Kingsley Publishers
London and Philadelphia

First published in 2007
by Jessica Kingsley Publishers
116 Pentonville Road
London N1 9JB, UK
and
400 Market Street, Suite 400
Philadelphia, PA 19106, USA

www.jkp.com

Copyright © David Kinchin 2007
Foreword copyright © Gordon Turnbull 2007

Library of Congress Cataloging in Publication Data
Kinchin, David.
   A guide to psychological debriefing : managing emotional decompression and post-traumatic stress disorder / David Kinchin.
      p. ; cm.
   ISBN 978-1-84310-492-6 (pb : alk. paper) 1. Post-traumatic stress disorder. 2. Crisis intervention (Mental health services) I. Title.
   [DNLM: 1. Stress Disorders, Post-Traumatic—therapy. 2. Crisis Intervention—methods. 3. Emergency Services, Psychiatric—methods. WM 170 K51g 2007]
   RC552.P67K5668 2007
   616.85'21—dc22

                                             2007014663

British Library Cataloguing in Publication Data
A CIP catalogue record for this book is available from the British Library

ISBN 978 1 84310 492 6

Printed and bound in Great Britain by
Athenaeum Press, Gateshead, Tyne and Wear

Contents

List of tables

List of figures

List of boxes

Foreword

I suppose that one of the most striking characteristics of human beings is their inquisitiveness: the need to make sense of the world around them. When that world goes 'topsy-turvy', it increases the need to do so – even more so when the changes are 'beyond usual experience'. The need to understand what has happened becomes imperative when survival has been threatened.

Also, being group-orientated creatures, the task of understanding events that have been life-threatening goes beyond the individual and becomes critical for the group, adding to the common store of protective knowledge for the 'next time'.

So, as soon as they could, human beings started to share critical experiences by talking about them to others, and this instinct became a natural, and informal, process. Debriefing is simply an extension of this natural state of affairs, which preserves the need to communicate information essential for survival, and there is nothing new about it: it is a human habit that is 'as old as the hills'.

In this book, David Kinchin is doing precisely that: he is describing his traumatic experiences to others, following a time-honoured tradition. He has 'been there', and he is giving his readers the benefit of his experience.

In the twentieth century, the need for a more formalised way to help people to process the imprint of psychological trauma had become evident and, looking back, it was most appropriate that this development first appeared in teams of 'trauma-seekers' – emergency service workers – who were the most likely individuals to be challenged by traumatic events on a day-to-day basis as part of their everyday working lives.

The 'trauma-seeking' teams greatly benefited from the introduction of 'Critical Incident Stress Debriefing' or 'Psychological Debriefing', as it was sometimes called, and the practice became very popular and widespread as a result. Emergency service personnel believed that debriefing helped to maintain morale and team cohesion in the face of adversity, and to help prevent the development of chronic trauma reactions.

But these 'trauma-seekers' represented the *secondary victims* of the events they became involved in. Debriefing was not perceived by them to be a 'treatment' but a natural way to help their constructed teams to process what they had absorbed while they were doing their work. It was only when the debriefing techniques were extended to help *primary victims* that their reported effectiveness in reducing the incidence of post-traumatic stress disorders needed to be evaluated. Effectively, what had been developed initially as a psychologically supportive technique for secondary victims was now being offered as a preventative treatment against the development of post-traumatic stress disorders for primary victims.

This new stage in the evolution of formalised debriefing quite correctly required controlled evaluation of the debriefing of the primary victims of trauma. Traumatic situations actually make this very difficult to do because of the wide range of factors that have to be taken into account. Let us take the timing of the debriefing as an example to demonstrate the complexity. Most of the emergency service personnel attending a critical incident would remain physically fit to attend a group debriefing within 24–72 hours of the event, but that would not necessarily be the case for a primary victim. It is much more likely for the latter to have been physically injured in the trauma and to be incapable of undertaking a useful debriefing so shortly afterwards. Also, a single formal debriefing will naturally extend into informal ongoing discussion within the team of secondary victims, whereas for the primary victim there may, indeed, be only one opportunity to try to process the imprint of the trauma with others.

The foregoing states the obvious, but what it also does is to make it plain that debriefing is a complicated process which will take time to understand.

In 1991, when I was in the Royal Air Force, I was given the opportunity to organise the first psychological debriefing of released British prisoners-of-war from the first Gulf War, and shortly afterwards of released British hostages from Beirut. We followed the guidelines recommended by the acknowledged 'gurus' in the field. We learned that it was important to be flexible and not to be afraid of innovation, that there was no precise formula for debriefing and that debriefing seemed to be a *re-entry* process.

We learned that their 'symptoms' seemed better to represent features of a survival reaction that were adaptive rather than pathological and seemed to be designed to facilitate recovery. Recurrent flashback memories of the trauma, although distressing, were also faithful memories that gave repeated opportunities to learn precisely what had happened, especially when shared in a group setting. We certainly gained a powerful impression that 'Emotional Decompression' prevented our people from becoming fixated on the sensory imprints of their individual traumatic experiences, and released them from becoming victims of their experiences for the rest of their lives.

In *A Guide to Psychological Debriefing*, David Kinchin pays special attention to setting up optimal conditions to facilitate Emotional Decompression. He takes into account that trauma reactions, primarily concerned with survival, are whole-system reactions, affecting both the body and mind. He also reminds us that the initial impact of the trauma is on physical structures in the brain, disrupting memory-processing capacity, which is designed to create space and time to heal.

In essence, David Kinchin's new book is about the exploration of ways to promote Emotional Decompression at an early stage after exposure to trauma in order to re-introduce a sense of safety and control and prevent chronic stress reactions. David Kinchin advocates Emotional Decompression, with all its facets, for both traumatised individuals and groups. He should know because he has 'been there'. We should all pay a great deal of attention to what he says in this book.

Professor Gordon Turnbull, MSc in Psychological Trauma, Department of Social and Communication Studies, University of Chester; and Consultant Psychiatrist, Capio Nightingale Hospital, London, and Ridgeway Hospital, Swindon, Wiltshire

CHAPTER ONE

Introduction to Post-Traumatic Stress Disorder

Traumatic events strike unexpectedly and turn everyday experiences upside down. They frequently destroy the belief that 'it could never happen to me'. In the aftermath of a disaster or event, people may believe that they were in the wrong place at the wrong time.

It is not only survivors of disasters who suffer trauma. Relatives, witnesses and emergency workers are also exposed. Once a person has experienced trauma, it may be extremely difficult for them to believe that their life can ever be the same again. Survival is not just to do with living – it is mostly to do with the *quality* of that living.

It is not certain why particular reactions occur to traumatic events, but they appear to be influenced by at least three important variables:

1. the traumatic nature of the incident

2. the character and personality of the individual involved – and what else is going on in their life at that moment

3. the preparation of the individual, and the support given before, during and after the event.

Trauma is defined in the *Oxford English Dictionary* as 'a powerful shock that may have long-lasting consequences'. The effects of trauma can be immediately overwhelming.

The standard résumé of what Post-Traumatic Stress Disorder (PTSD) is usually runs along the lines of:

Post-Traumatic Stress Disorder results when a person has been exposed to an event which may be outside the range of normal human experience: an event which would markedly distress almost anyone. It is the normal human response to an abnormal situation.

The experience could be a serious threat to life. It could be a serious threat or actual harm to one's children, partner or other close relative or friend. It could be the sudden destruction of one's home or community, or seeing another person who has been seriously injured or killed as the result of either an accident or physical violence. More recent evidence has shown that PTSD can result from sexual abuse or systematic bullying. PTSD goes further. The event only has to be perceived as traumatic by the victim or the witnesses.

In reality, the incident might not pose a serious threat to life, but, if the incident is genuinely considered to be life-threatening, then the victim has experienced an event outside the range of their normal experience. Some commentators have argued that there are now so many traumatic events occurring in our world – and these events are usually broadcast widely in the media – that not much is actually outside the range of human experience. It is suggested that the increase in PTSD is very much the product of modern living.

It could be argued that PTSD case numbers rise in ratio to advances in technology. The more advanced today's world becomes, the greater the scope for the existence of severe life stresses and traumatic situations. The more advanced our communications networks become, the more our minds are filled with plausible traumatic imagery. This is graphically illustrated by the way mobile phones played a significant part in the traumatic aspects of the 9/11 attack in the USA and the 7/7 bombings in London.

In the USA, people used their phones to call loved ones moments before they knew they themselves were going to die. For the recipients of these calls this was extremely traumatic. In London, the phones didn't work underground but they could still take very vivid pictures. News channels even advertise for people to use their mobile phones to take video clips of traumatic events – who sell them to the news organisations. We have all become trauma reporters.

The history of PTSD

PTSD, as a label, has only been around for a quarter of a century. Before that time, what people suffered was given a wide variety of different names (see Table 1.1).

Table 1.1 Historic names associated with what we now call PTSD

Name	Earliest reported use of this term
Soldier's Heart (Da Costa's Syndrome)	1862 American Civil War
Railway Spine	1866 John Erichsen
Neurastheniac (used more from 1917 when 'shell shock' was 'outlawed')	1869 G. Beard and E. Van Deusen
Disordered Action of the Heart (DAH) (from 1917 this was known as 'Effort Syndrome')	1891 Boer War
Shell Shock	1912 Dr Octave Laurent
War Neurosis	1916 World War I
Battle Neurosis	1940 World War II
Lack of Moral Fibre (LMF)	1940 Royal Air Force
Old Sergeant Syndrome	1950 Korean War
Combat Fatigue	1961 Vietnam War
Transient Situation Disturbance (TSD)	1968 Medical Journals
Buffalo Creek Syndrome	1972 From the disaster at Buffalo Creek
Battleshock	1982 Brigadier Peter Abraham
Post-Traumatic Stress Disorder (PTSD)	1979 Vietnam War Veterans
Gulf War Syndrome	1993 Media Reports

It is ironic that almost all these names come from situations of old soldiers returning from conflicts around the globe. The names, in part, are self-explanatory. For example, Soldier's Heart was linked to homesickness and not wanting to fight any more, and Railway Spine was derived from the aches and pains people suffered when riding ordinarily on a train. People conveniently forgot Railway Spine and thought trauma was restricted to acts of war. In the twenty-first century, however, trauma is a household word and PTSD is a much more common syndrome.

Large-scale disasters, either natural or man-made, will inevitably lead to a large number of people within one community being affected by PTSD. On 21 October 1966, a waste tip from a Welsh coal field slid down the side of a valley and demolished several houses and a village school. The incident at Aberfan killed 116 children and 28 adults (Austin 1967).

Five years later, a similar event happened in the USA. Thousands of tons of debris-filled muddy water burst through a makeshift mining company dam and roared through Buffalo Creek. In 1966, the people of Aberfan were considered to be suffering from 'severe shock'. In 1972, those in Buffalo Creek were labelled as suffering from a complex which became known journalistically as 'Buffalo Creek Syndrome'.

After seeing so many traumatised Vietnam veterans, the medical profession recognised that all victims of extremely traumatic events tended to exhibit similar behaviour and symptoms. Significant numbers of Vietnam veterans were displaying signs that all was not well with their lives. The war between the USA and Vietnam received bad publicity from many sources and even many Americans were opposed to the conflict. The war veterans' traumatic wartime experiences were adversely affecting their state of health. Upon returning home they were not welcomed as heroes. The combination of suffering severe trauma and experiencing such a negative reaction back home led some veterans to resort to drink, drugs and acts of violence.

Modern-day diagnosis

In 1980, the symptoms exhibited by these veterans, and those exhibited by civilian victims such as those at Buffalo Creek, were grouped under the diagnosis of PTSD for the first time. The definition, coded DSM-III, gave a name to the disorder and officially replaced such terms as shell shock; gross stress reaction; transient situation disturbance; and Buffalo Creek Syndrome. In 1994, this definition was amended (DSM-IV) and is now recognised worldwide. (DSM is the abbreviation for 'Diagnostic and Statistical Manual of Mental Disorders' and III and IV refer to editions three and four, all produced by the American Psychiatric Association (1980, 2000)).

The ICD-10 diagnosis of PTSD was produced by the World Health Organisation in 1993 so slightly predates DSM-IV. ICD-10 is a more relaxed definition and is sometimes preferred by trauma specialists as a diagnostic tool.

In 1996, the shooting incident in Dunblane shocked even the most hardened people. How it was possible for one man to walk into a school and shoot dead 16 children was hard to imagine. But that is exactly what 43-year-old Thomas Hamilton did on 13 March 1996. The world was deeply enraged by this incident, which, like the Aberfan disaster, lasted less than 20 minutes. The shock waves following this event continued for a long time. Britain, and the world, was becoming more aware of what traumatic events can do to individual people, to families and to communities. By the time of the Dunblane shootings, everyone was at least familiar with the initials PTSD even if they did not fully understand and appreciate the significance of the disorder.

This tragic shooting provided one of the largest incidences of 'trauma bonding'. There developed a bond between the residents of Dunblane and those living in Aberfan. The two disasters were separated by 30 years and 315 miles of countryside, but the two communities were united by an invisible 'trauma bond'. This bond is an understanding which exists between those who have witnessed or experienced a traumatic event.

The Boxing Day tsunami

On 26 December 2004, a word previously known only to students of geography came to the public attention – tsunami. It is estimated that approximately 300,000 people lost their lives as a result of the Boxing Day tsunami, which wreaked devastation along the coastlines of the Indian Ocean.

This catastrophe touched every continent, proving that the world is, indeed, a small place. The casualties from this giant tidal wave in Asia resulted in fatalities from the following European countries – Austria, Belgium, Britain, Croatia, Cyprus, the Czech Republic, Denmark, Estonia, Finland, France, Germany, Gibraltar, Greece, Ireland, Italy, Latvia, Lithuania, Luxembourg, Malta, Monaco, the Netherlands, Norway, Poland, Portugal, Russia, Spain, Sweden, Switzerland, Turkey and the Ukraine. It is astounding that a disaster around the Indian Ocean, which primarily affected Asian countries, could also have fatalities from 30 different European countries. Almost 16,000 European lives were lost in this one incident. The fact that so many different nationalities were affected by this disaster created extra problems. Different cultures have different approaches to counselling, debriefing and other forms of support. This really was a worldwide disaster.

The London bombings

On 7 July 2005, Britain was rocked by the terrorists' bombings in London. The 7/7 bombings occurred at a time when many people were familiar with the concept of PTSD, and yet the authorities still made blunders and mistakes in dealing with the traumatic aftermath of the incident. Potential victims were not offered the support of defusing and debriefing because there was squabbling and bickering about the measured value of these interventions. Victims were, in the main, left to seek treatment for themselves in a very ad hoc way.

It almost beggars belief that four men, with a budget of only a few hundred pounds and information gleaned from the internet, could be responsible for so much terror and trauma. Yet, despite all our knowledge of trauma and the consequences of being exposed to it, organisations were slow to respond to the demands of people seeking support. The official view and those of individual survivors differ tremendously as to the efficiency of the trauma services.

People are diagnosed using either the criteria of DSM-IV or ICD-10. While the diagnostic criteria within each system are similar, they are not the same (see Tables 1.2 and 1.3).

Table 1.2 Six criteria needed to meet a diagnosis of Post-Traumatic Stress Disorder

1. TRAUMA The person must be exposed to a traumatic event or events that involve actual or threatened death or serious injury, or threat to the physical integrity of self or others. The person's response must involve fear, helplessness or horror.

2. INTRUSIVE The event must be persistently relived by the person.

3. AVOIDANT The person must persistently avoid stimuli associated with the trauma.

4. PHYSICAL The person must experience persistent symptoms of increased arousal, or 'over-awareness'.

5. SOCIAL The disturbance must cause significant distress or impairment in social, occupational or other areas of functioning important to the person.

6. TIME Symptoms, linked to 2, 3 and 4 above, must have lasted at least one month.

Adapted from Diagnostic and Statistical Manual of Mental Disorders, 4th edition (DSM-IV), American Psychiatric Association (2000)

Having two definitions of PTSD, which are at odds with each other, can cause problems. There may be pressure on medical staff to refer to one diagnostic criteria (ICD-10) rather than the other (DSM-IV). There are political, financial and social reasons why this may occur, and it is left to the individual to reflect upon the consequences of this diagnostic battle.

The full diagnosis under DSM-IV allows for the definition and for three subtypes of PTSD. It also considers PTSD in children. The DSM-IV diagnosis is much stricter than the ICD-10 diagnosis. The DSM-IV description places much more emphasis on avoidance and emotional numbing symptoms. In addition, DSM-IV requires that the symptoms cause significant distress or interference with social or occupational functioning.

ICD-10 places no timescale on the onset of the disorder. DSM-IV requires that the symptoms must have persisted for at least one month. In the first month, according to DSM-IV, trauma survivors may be diagnosed as having *acute stress disorder* rather than full-blown PTSD.

Table 1.3 Five criteria needed to meet a diagnosis of Post-Traumatic Stress Disorder

1. The patient must have been exposed to a stressful event or situation (either short or long lasting) of exceptionally threatening or catastrophic nature, which would be likely to cause pervasive distress in almost anyone.

2. There must be persistent remembering or 'reliving' of the stressor in intrusive 'flashbacks', vivid memories, or recurring dreams, or in experiencing distress when exposed to circumstances resembling or associated with the stressor.

3. The patient must exhibit an actual or preferred avoidance of circumstances resembling or associated with the stressor, which was not present before exposure to the stressor.

4. Either of the following must be present:
   - inability to recall, either partially or completely, some important aspects of the period of exposure to the stressor
   - persistent symptoms of increased psychological sensitivity and arousal (not present before exposure to the stressor) shown by any two of the following: difficulty in falling or staying asleep; irritability or outbursts of anger; difficulty in concentrating; hypervigilance; exaggerated startle response.

5. Criteria 2, 3 and 4 must all be met within six months of the stressful event or the end of a period of stress. (For some purposes, onset delayed more than six months may be included but this should be clearly specified.)

Adapted from International Classification of Diseases, 10th edition (ICD-10), World Health Organisation (1993)

The demography of PTSD

The number of people who suffer from PTSD at any one time is equal to a little under 1½ per cent of the general population. In 1987, researchers carried out a survey of psychological disorders exhibited by the population of St Louis, Missouri (Hertzer 1987). A total of 2500 randomly selected residents were studied and 28 people were diagnosed as suffering from PTSD. Within those 28, the males cited only two types of event as a cause of the disorder: combat and witnessing someone hurt or dying. The most common event cited by the females was physical attack, including rape. Other events which were identified as triggering PTSD were being poisoned, and having a miscarriage. Major disasters accounted for none of the 28 cases. Although this research is now a little dated, it remains one of the most useful studies of PTSD in the general population.

Within some groups of society, the incidence of PTSD must be expected to be much higher than 1 per cent. Within the emergency services (fire, police and ambulance) and the armed forces (army, navy and air force), the incidence of PTSD can be as high as 30 per cent (Alexander 2001). It is a disturbing probability that out of every 100 police officers currently engaged in uniformed patrol duties in our towns and cities, up to 30 may be suffering from *some symptoms* of PTSD.

We should pause here just to clarify what that means. Even if 30 out of 100 police officers may be exhibiting symptoms linked to PTSD, that does not necessarily mean that 30 per cent of officers actually *have* PTSD. What it means is exactly what it says – that 30 officers have some symptoms of PTSD or may be in the acute stress disorder stage.

The disaster era

As with every other subject, post-traumatic stress has its own statistics to quote. Much of the work on the subject was brought about by the so-called 'disaster era' between 1985 and 1989. During those five years, 15 major incidents shook Britain, killing just over 1000 people and traumatising many more (see Table 1.4). These major incidents claimed considerable media attention and rightly so. But the only figures produced after each incident referred to fatalities. Without wishing to trivialise any death, it is true to say that dead people do not suffer from PTSD.

However, those who saw them die, or who were close to them either emotionally or physically at the time of their death, may well develop symptoms of PTSD. It is generally estimated that for every one death in an incident, there are likely to be at least ten people who are traumatised and go on to develop PTSD (the 'one in ten' rule). So the 15 disasters cited in the UK disaster era may well have produced around 11,000 cases of PTSD.

Table 1.4 The UK disaster era: 1985–1989

Date	Event	Deaths
11 May 1985	Bradford City Football Stadium fire	56
29 May 1985	Heysel Stadium crowd disturbance	56
22 Aug 1985	Manchester Airport fire	55
6 Mar 1987	*Herald of Free Enterprise* sank	187
19 Aug 1987	Hungerford shootings	16
8 Nov 1987	Enniskillen bombing	12
18 Nov 1987	King's Cross fire	31
6 Jul 1988	Piper Alpha oil rig fire	167
12 Dec 1988	Clapham rail crash	35
21 Dec 1988	Lockerbie plane crash	270
8 Jan 1989	East Midlands plane crash	47
4 Mar 1989	Purley train crash	6
15 Apr 1989	Hillsborough Stadium disaster	97
20 Aug 1989	*Marchioness* pleasure boat sank	51
22 Sept 1989	Deal Barracks bombing	11
	Total	1097

But major disasters account for only a fraction of the number of people who die as a result of accidents or violence. During the five years of 1985 to 1989, there were 108,862 accidental fatalities, of which just 1097 were linked to the 15 well-publicised major disasters. The rest of the fatalities were made up from car accidents, domestic accidents, crimes of violence and all the other incidents that account for about 56 deaths every day in the UK (1989 figures) and pass almost unnoticed by many of us. If the 'one in ten' rule is applied to all these deaths – that is, ten cases of PTSD for every fatality – then almost 1.1m people suffered from PTSD in Britain during that same five-year period. This figure is equal to about 1½ per cent of the total population.

PTSD high-risk groups

Of course, the 'one in ten' rule cannot be applied rigidly, but it can be used as a general guide. Any attempt to calculate more accurate figures would have to take into account that some events are more likely to traumatise people than others (see Table 1.5).

Table 1.5 Post-Traumatic Stress Disorder high-risk groups

Event	Risk (in per cent)
Shipwreck survivors	75
Bombing (terrorism) survivors	50
Sexual abuse victims	50
Rape victims	50
Combat victims	40
Hijack survivors	35
Victims of bullying	35
Emergency service staff	30
Air crash survivors	25
Car crash victims	20
General population	1.5

For example, rape victims have a 50 per cent risk of suffering PTSD following their ordeal, while car crash victims have only a 20 per cent chance. In addition, it would appear that some people may be more susceptible to PTSD than others, although there is no official agreement on this issue. These variables all have to be considered.

The 'one in ten' rule

Applying the 'one in ten' rule for the tsunami victims is a good indication that around 160,000 Europeans were affected by this Indian Ocean disaster. Many were holidaymakers who returned home numbed and shocked by what they saw. Support services in Europe were not equipped to cope with such a sudden influx of traumatised people and, although everyone did their best to greet people at airports and offer support when travellers had returned home, nobody could have anticipated such a disaster and such sky-high casualty figures. Not everyone will have come home and received a diagnosis of PTSD. Some will have become withdrawn and maybe diagnosed as depressed. Some may have taken to drink and/or drugs and become morose and grumpy. These people may turn to violence and crime – they may be caught drinking and driving – and their marriages may be under terrible strain.

Complex PTSD

In some instances, the individual may have experienced a prolonged series of stressful circumstances. An Iraq War veteran may have experienced several traumatic combat incidents over a period of weeks or months. A fire officer may deal with a run of house fires in which children have been fatally burned. In cases like these, the extensive cumulative stress is now more frequently referred to as 'Complex PTSD'.

A number of trauma survivors have experienced a range of different traumatic experiences during their lifetimes or prolonged traumas such as childhood sexual abuse or unauthorised imprisonment of some kind. Judith Herman, of Harvard University, first suggested the concept of Complex PTSD (Herman 1997) to describe the symptoms of long-term trauma.

Within the National Clinical Practice Guidelines (British Psychological Society 2005), reference is made to DESNOS (*disorders of extreme stress not otherwise specified*) and it would appear that, despite the best efforts of other researchers to clarify the situation regarding Complex PTSD, there is still a formal reluctance to accept that the disorder exists. However, it is suggested by some that Complex PTSD is present in many people who have been subjected to extreme and prolonged stresses.

Victims who have been held in a state of captivity and unable to flee can be said to be suffering from Complex PTSD. These groups will include those held in concentration camps or brothels, and those suffering long-term domestic violence, long-term physical abuse or child sexual abuse/exploitation. In addition, there is compelling evidence to suggest that some officers serving in the armed forces or the emergency services may actually be suffering from Complex PTSD, which has been brought about by regular exposure to a wide variety of traumatic stressors over a period of time.

No two people will have an identical reaction to one event. That is what makes us human. Two people who experience the same event together will react to it differently. If there are 200 people present, the variety of reactions is multiplied by that number; the only difference in a large group is that several people may have broadly similar reactions. Confronted by a traumatic situation, some will face it, others will move away. This reaction is referred to as 'fight or flight'. If the event is particularly traumatic, many will run the risk of developing PTSD.

What is normal?

Who can say what is normal? What can be said, without fear of contradiction, is that a person who is faced with an abnormal situation will react in some way to that situation. How the person reacts will depend on many other factors, such as previous experiences, mood at the time of the event and individual perception of the threat to personal safety.

Suppose you are leaving the cinema one evening and you come face-to-face with a youth. He brandishes a sharp knife under your nose and demands all your cash. It is likely that you first feel fear, then anger, then logic takes over and you reason that no amount of cash is worth a slashed face. The youth grins wildly, waving your money under your gaze to signify his victory, and runs off.

If, three weeks later, you are leaving a football match and someone rushes up to you waving your forgotten coat, your first reaction may be one of panic. Your mind, briefly, links the two events because some aspects of the first traumatic event have been repeated in the second, friendly, incident. Most people familiar with the circumstances of the robbery will see your initial panic reaction as normal. People witnessing the second event, not knowing about the robbery, might consider your initial panic as rather unusual. It is all a matter of perception and understanding.

A psychological phenomenon

PTSD is an emotional condition, from which it is possible to make a completely satisfactory recovery.

The most distressing symptom of PTSD is the reliving of the traumatic event, whether you want to or not. This re-experiencing may take the form of recurrent nightmares or daytime flashbacks. In either case, victims are troubled by vivid, repetitive pictures of the trauma. Sometimes these pictures are so real that they start to behave as though the event were happening all over again. This re-experiencing may last only a few seconds, but it might last hours or even days initially. Quite often, people are fully aware of what is happening but can do nothing to control the situation. The flashbacks can occur with distressing frequency, adding fuel to the totally erroneous belief that the person is 'going mad'.

The memory of the event is usually in picture form. Sounds and smells can act as a trigger to start the picture sequence. Former Middle East hostage Terry Waite tells how the sound of masking tape being ripped from the roll triggered terrible memories of his days in captivity (Waite 1993). Chained and blindfolded in a tiny cell, he was frequently moved from one 'safe house' to another. Before every move, he was bound with masking tape; even his mouth and eyes were covered. It is little wonder that a harmless and familiar sound to many should be such a traumatic trigger for him.

Because these vivid flashbacks are so unpredictable, victims find themselves at a disadvantage. Former friends and colleagues may feel insecure and unsure about how to react. Canteen chatterers may start to label the victim as a 'nutter' or a 'head case'. These labels are not appropriate to anyone and they are certainly not appropriate descriptions of a

PTSD victim. Unfortunately, the labels tend to stick. Victims start to panic. They avoid situations or activities which are likely to trigger the images. Their lifestyle changes and they start to lose contact with other people.

This spiral of events may lead to feelings of depression and anxiety. Untreated, this can have dangerous and far-reaching consequences. Resultant poor attendance at the workplace may result in unemployment, while irritability often adds strain to all personal relationships. All this, combined with possible uncontrollable and violent outbursts during periods when the victim is re-experiencing the trauma, can add up to an unbearable life. Things cannot continue in this way for long.

In seeking medical help, the last straw for PTSD victims is to picture themselves as mentally irredeemable cases doomed to spend the rest of their lives in a Dickensian-style institution for the insane. A grim picture indeed. This is a false expectation, but one common to many PTSD sufferers. They are not mad, but they do require specialised help and loving support.

If every person who ever experienced a traumatic event always suffered from PTSD, the disorder would become almost as common as colds or flu. Clearly not everyone is affected to that same degree. Why?

Imagine two little rocks sitting on the beach at the seaside. One is made of sandstone and the other is made of granite. Both rocks are exposed to the same weather, the same wind and rain. Both rocks are smashed around by the same waves and tides. However, the rock made of granite will stand up to this battering of the elements far better than the piece of sandstone. Human beings are a little like the rocks. Some are made up of sandstone and others are like granite. The problem is that sometimes people take on the characteristics of granite and at other times they take on the characteristics of sandstone, and it all depends upon what else is going on in their lives at the time. It is almost impossible to know who is made from which stone.

Research studies that have examined the causes of PTSD are scarce. It is still difficult to identify those most likely to be affected, and those at greatest risk. Very little of the research is conclusive and any figures quoting a person's 'PTSD risk' are likely to be contested by various bodies having a vested interest in either underestimating or overestimating the figures.

The two Gulf Wars

Ministry of Defence departments will play down the psychological casualty figures. When asked about PTSD cases in 1994, the Ministry of Defence in London claimed that only 68 British combat troops received any form of psychiatric treatment as a direct result of the first Gulf War. In 1991, the independent group Trauma After Care Trust (TACT) claimed the figure to be at least 13,000. The reality has proved to be far worse than either of these early predictions.

By the summer of 2006, in the Iraq War, over 130 British soldiers have been killed, a small number compared with the American losses. American support services have anticipated vast numbers of traumatised soldiers returning home from Iraq, but British armed forces medical staff suggest that British soldiers are not really expected to be traumatised by what they experience. The expectation in the USA was that soldiers *would* probably be traumatised. The expectation in the UK is that soldiers would probably *not* be traumatised. This difference in expectations says a lot about the two different cultures and their acceptance and understanding of any psychological disorder. This is to do with perception and understanding of the situation.

Following the first Gulf War, a number of servicemen and women grouped together in an attempt to take the Ministry of Defence to court. This 'class action', as it is known, was doomed to fail for a variety of reasons, but one or two useful comments came from the judge in this case.

Mr Justice Owen commented in the summing up of the 'PTSD class action' in 2003: 'Psychiatric/psychological disorder…was seen to be a sign of weakness, which if revealed, would expose an individual to ridicule, and would be the "kiss of death" to a military career' (Owen 2003, p.166). The consequence of this blindingly obvious comment by the judge in this well-documented case is that far too many men and women try to hide their troubles and suffer in silence for fear of losing their career.

What really beggars belief is that way back in World War I Lord Moran based upon his own experiences, argued:

> Even prodigal youth has to husband its resources. Likewise, in the trenches a man's own will power was his capital and he was always spending, so that wise and thrifty company officers watched the expenditure of every penny lest their men went bankrupt. When their capital was done, they were finished. (Moran 1945, p.69)

Sadly these words have not been fully appreciated down the years and it would appear that every major conflict requires some sort of 're-inventing of the wheel' when it comes to understanding the psychological consequences of war. Even in the twenty-first century there is a severe stigma attached to suffering from PTSD in Britain, particularly in the Armed Forces. This stigma is also extended to those in the emergency services and to any profession in which people have a duty of care towards others (e.g. nurses, counsellors and teachers).

PTSD is selective

PTSD is selective. Not everyone is affected. Unfortunately, it is not possible to predict who will be affected by this disorder or when. There are some indications, however, that particular groups of people may be more susceptible to the disorder than others. Women are more susceptible than men. People who possess an introverted personality may be at slightly greater risk. A family history of anxiety or depression may be a contributing factor. These ideas are based upon very limited research studies purely because PTSD is such an impossibly difficult disorder to monitor.

It appears likely that a person with pre-existing difficulties, which create a stressful lifestyle, may have already stretched their psychological and emotional defences to near breaking point. The life-threatening trauma will be the final straw.

Carers and rescue workers can have their risks reduced by careful training and preparation to expect trauma. Once a traumatic event has been experienced, the personnel involved must be fully, and professionally, counselled in a procedure known as 'Psychological Debriefing'

(Parkinson 1997). In more recent times, it has been suggested that the name of this procedure be changed because 'debriefing' means different things to different people. Some commentators now describe the procedure as 'Emotional Decompression'.

Traumatic events

Over the years there have been many events which have resulted in significant numbers of people being traumatised. You will be familiar with some of these more recent experiences. Each large-scale event attracted immense media attention at the time but eventually the interest waned and those who were affected were abandoned by the media. They were of no further interest.

However, those traumatised by these events continued to suffer from the aftershocks of the trauma and will carry traumatic scar tissue for the rest of their lives. In order to chart the progress that has been made in understanding PTSD, it may be useful to examine a number of the events shown in Table 1.6.

These events are commented upon in chronological order so that you can see something of the picture of growth in understanding of PTSD as related to the traumas and tragedies. The last two incidents have been included specifically to indicate that trauma isn't just limited to major disasters. Local small-scale events can be equally traumatic.

World War I

22 April 1915 saw the death of a soldier. He was shot dead. At just 22 years of age, Private Albert Troughton came to the end of his life. He was shot by his own side, shot as a coward because he would not fight. The evidence for this was that he had managed to return to his own lines, while all his comrades were either dead or captured. It was suggested that he had lost his nerve. The words 'shell shock' were not used in relation to Private Albert Troughton, but there can be little doubt that anyone who witnessed the killing of all his friends at Ypres would be seriously traumatised, to use modern-day language.

Table 1.6 Traumatic events and related research studies

Event	Date	Significance	Research
World War I	22 April 1915	Soldier shot for cowardice	Elton 2005; Finer 2006; Jones and Wessely 2005; Moran 1945
Aberfan	21 October 1966	Before knowledge of PTSD	Austin 1967; Lacey 1972; Miller 1974; Raphael 1986
Buffalo Creek	26 February 1972	First modern study of the effects of trauma	Cohen 1991; Erikson 1976; Green *et al.* 1991; James, Titchener and Kapp 1976; Stern 1976
Chowchilla	15 July 1976	First study of children and PTSD	Raphael 1986; Saylor 1993; Terr 1981, 1983
Central London	7 July 2005	Terrorist bombings of transport network	No research has yet been published
Carmarthen Bay	21 June 2006	Freak fishing accidents	Too recent to have been included in any research or publication

The following poem was written by Siegfried Sassoon (1886–1967).

Suicide in the Trenches

I knew a simple soldier boy
Who grinned at life in empty joy,
Slept soundly through the lonesome dark,
And whistled early with the lark.

In winter trenches, cowed and glum,
With crumps and lice and lack of rum,

He put a bullet through his brain.
No one spoke of him again.

You smug-faced crowds with kindling eye
Who cheer when soldier lads march by,
Sneak home and pray you'll never know
The hell where youth and laughter go.

(Copyright © Siegfried Sassoon by kind permission
of the Estate of George Sassoon)

In the Washington Post newspaper on 8 June 2006, Jonathan Finer
wrote about the plight of US troops in Iraq:

> Composed of soldiers who are also trained as therapists, the combat
> stress teams are often sent immediately to debrief soldiers in the hours
> after a patrol, firefight or bomb attack.

US troops have trained therapists within their number to support
collagues who are distressed and stressed by war.
Finer went on:

> The most comprehensive psychological study of Iraq war veterans –
> completed in 2004 as the insurgency was still gaining strength – found
> that about 18 per cent suffered from post-traumatic stress disorder
> (PTSD), a constellation of physical and psychological symptoms first
> diagnosed among soldiers who serviced in Vietnam.

If 18 per cent of US soldiers are traumatised, just imagine how high a
percentage of British soldiers in 1915 standing in the trenches at Ypres
waiting to 'go over the top' must have been traumatised.

A novel by comedian Ben Elton, *The First Casualty*, deals very sympathetically with this problem and with the whole issue of trauma and war.
It is a surprisingly good read and not the sort of book you might expect
this type of text to be recommending.

Aberfan

Friday 21 October 1966 was the last school day before half-term. The
weather was depressingly misty but the children and staff at Pantglas
Junior School, in Aberfan, South Wales, were all looking forward to the

brief holiday (Austin 1967). Two hundred and forty boys and girls made their way to school. The youngest was 4½ and the eldest was 11. Pantglas was a happy school and most of the parents in Aberfan had known it as children themselves; they had learned their first lessons within its well-built brick and stone walls.

09.15   School has settled down. The teacher is about to mark the register. A call of 'dinner children' is heard from the corridor. Some go to pay their dinner shillings in the hall. Two are spotted by the headmistress, Miss Jennings, and sent to the senior school with a message.

09.18   An avalanche crashes through the school. It kills one of the two children on their way to the senior school. A black, wet mass slurps through a classroom, and fills Miss Jennings' study. She's 64, due to retire at the end of term. Next door, Mrs Bates and 33 children, aged 10 and 11, all die.

09.29   All 11 of the school soccer team, who had won their match against Troedyrhiw Junior School 3–2 the afternoon before, are killed.

A waste tip had slid down the side of the valley and demolished several houses and the school. The incident killed 116 children and 28 adults. In just 14 minutes, every person in the community had been permanently scarred by a disaster which touched the hearts of millions (Miller 1974).

This disaster is vividly recalled by many Britons because it was covered by television crews who arrived on the scene. The full horror and traumatic consequences of the disaster were screened in millions of homes. The first news flash was broadcast on radio at 10.30am. It brought reporters by the dozen as well as television services for the first big outside broadcast disaster coverage in the history of British television.

In 1966, nobody talked about PTSD. Nobody understood the effects of trauma on children, or parents, or rescuers (Lacey 1972). People coped as best they could and, while the nation watched on TV, the community of Aberfan started to pick up the pieces of their lives.

Aberfan made the headlines for quite a long time. The resulting inquiry was also big news. People were looking for somebody to blame and the Coal Board was hot favourite to fill that role. Nothing at all was known of PTSD but people in the village of Aberfan, and folk from surrounding villages, rallied round and supported each other. They were all in the same boat – they had all witnessed the consequences of this terrible event and they were instantly well aware that the school – the focal building in a village society – was destroyed completely.

Buffalo Creek

On Saturday 26 February 1972, an enormous slag dam gave way and unleashed 132m gallons of water and black mud on the Buffalo Creek valley in southern West Virginia. The mining hamlets of Becco and Pardee and the town of Saunders were almost totally destroyed. The disaster resulted in 126 deaths and it left 4000 people homeless. Many of the dead were women and children. Like the Aberfan tragedy, the actual incident lasted less than a quarter of an hour and the consequences were equally devastating (Erikson 1976).

Adults and children who survived referred to the disaster as 'the end of time' or 'the end of everything', and claimed that 'no one who was not there could ever really know what it was like' (James *et al.* 1976). Victims were haunted by visual memories of the event as they struggled with the emotional guilt, the drowning of relatives and friends, and witnessing blackened bodies that were uncovered for weeks after the flood. For these communities, the impossible had happened.

The shock was overwhelming and an outlook of pessimism, emptiness and hopelessness dominated the region. Such comments as 'nothing counts any more' and 'what's the use of anything?' became common. Survivors felt guilt for having survived. Anxiety, depression and feelings of inadequacy were commonplace.

In 1966, the people of Aberfan were considered to be suffering from 'severe shock'. In 1972, those in Buffalo Creek were labelled as suffering from a complex which became known journalistically as 'Buffalo Creek Syndrome'. Traumatic reactions were found in *80 per cent* of the survivors of the Buffalo Creek disaster, and many victims were still psychologically scarred two years after the event (Erikson 1976).

This was six years after Aberfan – it was during the time of the Vietnam War – and it was in the USA where, historically, people are better at getting support for themselves from therapists. 'Everyone has their own shrink' was the order of the day.

Help and support in the form of therapists did descend upon the villages around Buffalo Creek but that didn't prevent people suffering the nightmares and sleepless nights which we now link to PTSD. It was clear that something was wrong within the community and that people were exhibiting odd symptoms. Not everyone was the same but there was a pattern of symptoms emerging. Therapists came to the conclusion that these people were suffering from Buffalo Creek Syndrome, which was a fair enough assumption. The problem came when other disasters followed on from this, and those people suffered similar symptoms to the people in Buffalo Creek. This was more than something which was linked to one little community in outback southern West Virginia!

Chowchilla

At 4.05pm on Thursday 15 July 1976, 26 children who had enrolled in the Alview Dairyland Summer School, Chowchilla, California, were kidnapped. The children, aged 5–14 years, were travelling in a bus when three masked men stopped it at gunpoint. The children were transferred to two white vans and driven for about 11 hours before they were transferred to a 'hole in the ground' which was later found to be a buried truck trailer. The group spent 16 hours inside this buried trailer until two of the oldest boys managed to dig themselves out. The group had suffered a 27-hour ordeal.

The names and ages of the children are copied in Box 1.1 from a reproduction of a sheet of paper used by the kidnappers so the ages and spellings of names may not be accurate (Baugh and Morgan 1978). Reproducing the names here is a deliberate attempt to make reading about the kidnapping a much more personal experience. These are real people (children in this instance) who have been subjected to a real life trauma and have been put in fear of their lives.

**Box 1.1 Names and ages of children kidnapped
in Chowchilla in 1976**

Ronica Andre, 5	Sherry Heinzly, 7
Lisa Artery, 9	Mike Marshall, 14
Lisa Barletta, 12	Jody Mathony, 10
Jennifer Brown, 9	Lora Ozzi, 5
Jeth Brown, 11	Andrea Park, 8
Irene Creal, 12	Larry Park, 6
Stella Creal, 6	Barbara Parker, 8
Charly Daniels, 10	Becky Reynolds, 8
John Easterbrook, 8	Judy Reynolds, 13
Andy Gonzales, 8	Angela Robinson, 9
Robby Gonzales, 11	Mischel Robinson, 11
July Greham, 7	Linda Torreo, 10
Jody Hefington, 10	Cindy Van Hon, 7

Just prior to the kidnapping the bus had already delivered five children to their homes and these children were also traumatised by 'just missing' being kidnapped:

Edward Gregori, 5	Nancy Tripp, 11
Debbie Tripp, 6	Susan Zylstra, 7
Miles Tripp, 8	

Immediately after the event, when the children had been re-united with their parents and friends, a meeting was arranged for the parents to speak to a specialist mental health centre physician. This man told the children's parents that he confidently predicted that only one of the 26 children would be emotionally affected by the experience.

The parents were naturally reluctant to admit it was their child who was affected. Consequently, there was a delay of over five months before families started asking for help. When psychiatrist Lenore Terr met with the 23 children who still lived in Chowchilla six months after the event, she concluded that *all* those she interviewed were severely traumatised (Terr 1981, 1983).

The Chowchilla incident was significantly different from the disasters at Aberfan and Buffalo Creek. First, the trauma lasted many hours compared to just a few minutes. Second, the group consisted of children only. Third, and perhaps most importantly, there were no fatalities.

Researchers were keen to examine the children of Chowchilla and to explore their understanding of trauma. Four years after the incident, all 23 children were interviewed by Terr and her team and all continued to exhibit some signs of trauma. This included one child, Susan Zylstra, who had been let off the bus moments before the kidnapping. She was traumatised by the event (even though she was not kidnapped) and by the police interview conducted immediately after the incident.

This kidnapping happened in the middle of the Bicentenary Year in the USA. Lenore Terr was the therapist who appeared to spend much of her career researching into how these children, and their families, coped with being held hostage for 27 hours. She followed these children for some years, undertaking her research and writing papers and reports on what she found. Chowchilla was unique in that it was a major event in the history of the development of PTSD and yet there were *no fatalities* on this occasion. If there are no fatalities, then how do you apply the 'one in ten' rule to estimate the number of PTSD victims? You can't.

By 1976, there were the beginnings of some research into the Vietnam War veterans. Terr realised that she might be on to something here. This Chowchilla incident traumatised almost everyone who was directly involved in it – it also traumatised some people who were not directly involved but were on the edge of events. This was something more than just Buffalo Creek Syndrome and I think Terr made it her lifelong crusade to follow the children as they grew and to study the way they developed.

Central London
On 7 July 2005, a total of 52 people were killed during a terrorist attack on London. The day will be remembered for spectacularly high levels of anxiety and panic because nobody knew when or where the next bomb would explode. A total of four devices were exploded, three on Underground trains and one on a London bus.

The four suicide bombers (who also died) timed their attack to perfection by picking a day when 1500 Metropolitan Police officers were redeployed to the G8 Summit in Scotland. It was also the end of the morning rush-hour and people were still going to work, so the travel networks were very busy.

The event was broadcast on the television news as it happened and conflicting reports were given by different news stations. The overall picture was one of chaos and panic. Fifty-four state schools were closed that day because staff and pupils were unable to reach the premises. Mobile phone networks across London were either jammed or switched off as millions of calls were attempted at the same time.

Following these bombings, a full inquiry, under the chairmanship of Richard Barnes, was set up and reported its findings on 5 June 2006. The report blamed poor communications networks for much of the confusion which occurred that day. Recommendations made in connection with the Underground communication system following the King's Cross fire (18 years earlier) had still not been implemented and people at ground level could not talk to rescuers and those trapped underground.

Staggeringly, the report showed that potentially hundreds, perhaps thousands, of dazed and slightly injured people wandered away from the scenes without providing their details to anyone in authority. These people are unlikely to have been offered any sort of support or trauma counselling and the report found this unacceptable.

There is little doubt that the London bombings of 7 July will provide psychologists with heaps of research material in the years to come. It will be the UK version of the 9/11 attacks which took place in the USA in 2001. The 52 people who died were a mix of ages, sexes, nationalities, faiths. The 23 men and 29 women have become famous for all the wrong reasons, and their families and friends will have to come to terms with that. There were mothers and fathers killed, and sons and daughters died in the biggest disaster to strike the UK for many years.

The survivors of the bombings will be equally well mixed. Included in the survivors are the men and women of the emergency services who are likely to suffer the psychological consequences of this series of four bombs. They bravely went underground to assist the walking wounded to escape, then spent a more focused time dealing with individuals who were trapped or more seriously injured and needed more prolonged attention.

History has proved that some of the police, ambulance and fire officers who assisted survivors of the Moorgate tube train crash in 1975 are still suffering with nightmares and flashbacks well over 30 years after the incident. In 1975, very little was known about PTSD and the psychological consequences of dealing with trauma.

In 2005, there was no excuse for allowing anyone to escape the net and to leave the scene without giving their details so that debriefers, counsellors and psychologists could offer necessary assistance and then monitor recovery from this traumatic experience. Individual people were left to fend for themselves and anecdotal evidence suggests that local GPs were not terribly sympathetic to their plight and played down any slight possibility that they might go on to suffer PTSD.

Carmarthen Bay

On 21 June 2006, two men died in a fishing accident. The men had been enjoying an afternoon fishing off the rocks at Mwnt in Ceredigion. In addition and nearby, a yachtsman died after he was hit by the sail boom on his boat. Also on the same day, a 62-year-old man was washed into the sea while enjoying a coastal walk in Pembrokeshire. His body was washed up on the rocks near a breakwater at Fishguard.

Three different incidents resulted in four fatalities. All these activities – fishing, sailing, coastal walking – are deemed to be safe by most of us and yet they can end in tragedy and death. These three events were devastating for the families involved.

These incidents illustrate just how many different people can become involved in a trauma: the telephone operators who received the 999 calls; the police, coast guard, lifeboat and helicopter staff who became involved; there might have been a doctor or an undertaker called; and finally, there were the members of the general public who may have become involved in the trauma as it unfolded. When everything is done and dusted, loved ones and friends are left to come to terms with the unexpectedness and the consequences of what has happened.

None of these incidents made the national news programmes – they were not of major interest. This doesn't make the impact of these events any less traumatic. For those who were involved, each was a major event. It will perhaps be the most terrible and traumatic event of their lives to date. Therefore, it is important that those involved are made aware of the possibilities and consequences of what they have experienced, and this can be done by defusing, by debriefing and by professional support.

These are local incidents, affecting only a few people. It doesn't require an Aberfan, or a Buffalo Creek or a Chowchilla to cause trauma. It happens all around us every day. Therefore, the likelihood of having PTSD is equally common. PTSD is something which most people will experience at least once in their lifetime.

These traumatic stories are not placed here simply to distress you. There is a purpose to all this. It is vitally important that you appreciate the wide range of events that can result in people suffering from PTSD. These events have all been well publicised and many are also well documented and researched.

However, there are also the very personal and private events which don't raise any newspaper headlines and don't appear on the national TV news. Rape, sexual assault, an incident of bullying and abuse – these are all kept very quiet because the victims shun publicity. Local road traffic accidents don't even warrant the attendance of the police – drivers exchange names and addresses – but the passengers may have felt that they were fast approaching the end of their life: they could see it coming. For them the *minor accident* on the road is a *major trauma* in their minds. It is sometimes months or even years before they can get inside a car again.

Statistically the major events are not very significant. There are many more minor events which result in just as much trauma for those who are involved. Remember the 'one in ten' rule. For every one fatality there are ten people who are traumatised. These include witnesses, bystanders, emergency service staff, hospital casualty staff and anyone else who has been involved in the event. However, this 'one in ten' rule doesn't work if there are no fatalities! We tend to measure the significance of any traumatic event by the number of fatalities and that can often be a very misleading way of assessing things.

The London bombings of 7 July show graphically how a major incident sucks people into the trauma. Hundreds, probably thousands, of people were traumatised by the four bombs which exploded on that day. Some will have gone on to develop PTSD as a result of what they experienced.

During the time which has elapsed since 1966, our understanding of trauma, traumatic stress and PTSD has grown substantially. Many of these incidents have been headline news in the media. They have drawn the attention of the public and, in consequence, the support and interest of caring professionals and researchers. Large-scale traumas are well documented. Smaller traumatic events in which perhaps only one or two people are involved (such as Carmarthen Bay) happen every day. Road accidents, accidents at school or work, sudden deaths due to illness, suicides, rapes and instances of abuse or bullying happen in small communities throughout the world. Individually, they may appear to have minimal impact but combined they have a far greater impact than any shooting or mud slide or boat sinking.

Research into the traumatic consequences of road traffic accidents has been undertaken by a number of bodies including the Oxford Road Accident Group (ORAG). ORAG looked at 188 consecutive road accident victims admitted to the John Radcliffe Hospital following 184 different road accidents (Mayou, Bryant and Duthie 1993). The victims were interviewed a year after the accidents and it was found that over 10 per cent were suffering from PTSD symptoms. The researchers concluded that psychiatric symptoms were frequent after major and less severe road accident injuries. It further concluded that PTSD symptoms were both common and disabling.

Bibliography

Alexander, D. (2001) 'Ambulance personnel and critical incidents.' *British Journal of Psychiatry 178*, 76–81.

American Psychiatric Association (1980) *Diagnostic and Statistical Manual of Mental Disorders*, 3rd edition. Washington, DC: American Psychiatric Association.

American Psychiatric Association (2000) *Diagnostic and Statistical Manual of Mental Disorders*, 4th edition. Washington, DC: American Psychiatric Association.

Austin, T. (1967) *Aberfan: The Story of a Disaster.* London: Hutchinson.

Baugh, J.W. and Morgan, J. (1978) *Why Have They Taken our Children?* New York: Delacorte Press.

British Psychological Society (2005) *Post-Traumatic Stress Disorder: The Management of PTSD in Adults and Children in Primary and Secondary Care (NICE Guidelines).* London: Royal College of Psychiatrists.

Cohen, D. (1991) *Aftershock: The Psychological and Political Consequences of Disaster.* London: Paladin.

Elton, B. (2005) *The First Casualty.* London: Bantam Press.

Erikson, K.T. (1976) *Everything in its Path: Destruction of Community in Buffalo Creek Flood.* New York: Simon and Schuster.

Finer, J. (2006) 'Frontline care for "at risk" soldiers.' *Washington Post*, June 8.

Green, B.L., Korol, M., Grace, M., Vary, M., Leonard, A.C. and Gleser, G.C. (1991) 'Children and disaster: age, gender and parental effects on PTSD symptoms.' *Journal of the American Academy of Child and Adolescent Psychiatry 30*, 945–951.

Herman, J.I. (1997) *Trauma and Recovery.* New York: Basic Books.

Hertzer, J. (1987) 'Post-traumatic stress disorder in the general population: Findings of the Epidemiologic Catchment Area Survey.' *New England Journal of Medicine 317*, 1630–1634.

James, L., Titchener, M.D. and Kapp, F.C. (1976) 'Family and character change at Buffalo Creek.' *American Journal of Psychiatry 133*, 3, 295–299.

Jones, E. and Wessely, S. (2005) *Shell Shock to PTSD.* New York: Psychology Press.

Lacey, G. (1972) 'Observations on Aberfan.' *Journal of Psychosomatic Research 16*, 257–260.

Mayou, R., Bryant, B. and Duthie, R. (1993) 'Psychiatric consequences of road traffic accidents.' *British Medical Journal 307*, 647–651.

Miller, J. (1974) *Aberfan: A Disaster and its Aftermath.* London: Constable.

Moran, W.C. (1945) *The Anatomy of Courage.* London: Collins.

Owen, Mr Justice (2003) 'Multiple claimants versus the Ministry of Defence.' Typescript judgement of the PTSD class action.

Parkinson, F. (1997) *Critical Incident Debriefing.* London: Souvenir Press.

Raphael, B. (1986) *When Disaster Strikes: A Handbook for the Caring Professionals.* London: Unwin Hyman.

Saylor, C.F. (ed.) (1993) *Children and Disasters.* New York: Plenum Press.

Stern, G.M. (1976) *The Buffalo Creek Disaster.* New York: Vintage Books.

Terr, L.C. (1981) 'Psychic trauma in children: Observations following the Chowchilla school-bus kidnapping.' *American Journal of Psychiatry 138,* 1, 14–19.

Terr, L.C. (1983) 'Chowchilla revisited: The effects of psychic trauma four years after a school-bus kidnapping.' *American Journal of Psychiatry 140,* 12, 1543–1550.

Waite, T. (1993) *Taken on Trust.* London: Hodder and Stoughton.

World Health Organisation (WHO) (1993) *The ICD-10 Classification of Mental and Behavioural Disorders: Diagnostic Criteria for Research.* Geneva: WHO.

CHAPTER TWO

Introduction to Psychological Debriefing

In 1964, three eminent psychologists went head-to-head in an attempt to demonstrate their approach to dealing with a client who presented herself for counselling. Entitled *Three Approaches to Psychotherapy*, this footage very quickly became known among counsellors as the 'Gloria Tape'. Gloria was the willing guinea pig for Frederick (Fritz) Pearls, Albert Ellis and Carl Rogers as each in turn attempted to counsel Gloria about the guilt she suffered having lied to her nine-year-old daughter, Pamela, about being sexually active subsequent to her divorce.

Three Approaches to Psychotherapy was a 'must watch' film for many trainee counsellors in the 1960s as each of these great men demonstrated in turn their own theories at the expense of the luckless Gloria. Even today, many who work in the training of counsellors speak fondly of the 'Gloria Tape', and it is sad to note that the woman at the centre of the excitement, who died in 1979, failed to realise the impact she had made on many young counsellors.

In the field of psychological debriefing, there is no Pearls, Ellis or Rogers to lead the field and promote their own model of debriefing in the same self-serving style of the 1960s, but there are other contenders. I wonder, very wickedly, what would happen if Mitchell, Dyregrov and Parkinson were each offered one quarter of a traumatised group of soldiers and given 30 minutes to film their approach to debriefing! Of course, a fourth group would receive no debriefing at all from Wessely! This would perhaps be the only way to end the rhetoric of the 'debriefing debate' which has smouldered for years around the world.

In the real world, 'Three Approaches to Debriefing' is never going to happen as a film, because it wouldn't have any real value and it most certainly would not be considered ethically correct. Nevertheless, it is important to understand the history of debriefing and to explore the models of those most prominent in this field of trauma care (see Table 2.1) before moving forward and examining Emotional Decompression as a simple but effective form of psychological debriefing that can be provided, even by peers.

Table 2.1 Historic names for what is today called 'Psychological Debriefing'

Name	Originator	Date
Critical Incident Debriefing (CID)	Mitchell	1975
Critical Incident Stress Debriefing (CISD)	Mitchell	1983
Multiple Stressor Debriefing (MSD)	Armstrong	1991
Post Office Model	Tehrani	1994
Psychological Debriefing (PD)	Parkinson	1997
	Dyregrov	2001
Early Intervention	Psychological Society Working Party	2001
TRiM (Trauma Risk Management)	Royal Marines Model	2002
Emotional Decompression (ED)	Kinchin	2004

Psychological debriefing suffered from a bad press during the period 1994–2001, and a number of people spoke out against the principle that debriefing was a useful tool. In the late 1990s, I was among those people who were rather sceptical about debriefing. I have now changed my view completely.

Debriefing is not a cure for Post-Traumatic Stress Disorder (PTSD), or an injection against the development of the disorder. Neither does it suggest that all who are involved in a debrief are suffering, or will suffer, from the consequences of a trauma. It assumes that most people will cope after a traumatic incident, but that they will recover more quickly if they have a structured procedure to follow which helps them to talk about what has happened. I think my previous scepticism about the principle of debriefing was more to do with the practicalities surrounding the debrief than with the debrief itself.

Do debriefs stick to the rules?

It was generally agreed that debriefing should take place around 36–72 hours after the incident. People's working hours (including shift patterns and days off) and overtime arrangements should be taken into account, but the debriefing should run without any breaks (other than brief comfort breaks). This belief has now changed considerably and will be explored later in this text.

Who does the debrief?

The debriefer may belong to the organisation concerned, or may be independent and contacted through an agency. Increasingly, organisations are training their own personnel as debriefers, and this has advantages and disadvantages. The main advantage is that internally supplied debriefers will know the workings of the organisation very well. The disadvantage is that issues of confidentiality and professionalism may be compromised.

Anecdotal evidence suggests that many trauma victims prefer to be debriefed by someone who is not known to them, which usually means a person from outside their organisation. Paradoxically, many organisations prefer to have their own people carry out the debriefing because it is cheaper, and because they feel they have more control over the way the debrief is conducted. The feelings of those needing the debrief are not always taken into consideration. It should be remembered that the cheapest debriefing may not necessarily be the one with the best outcome.

A number of eminent researchers insist that a minimum of two debriefers should be present at any debriefing. However, the debriefing can be for one or more potential victims.

Where is the debrief conducted?

The debrief should take place in a quiet, comfortable venue. Telephones, mobile phones, pagers and all other outside interference should be banned from the room. Refreshments should be available from the very beginning of the time set aside.

Who is invited to the debrief?

This is always a problem. If a debrief becomes too big, it is ineffective. However, if people are missing, it is also ineffective. It is finding this compromise between the size and effectiveness of the group that forms my greatest misgiving about the exercise.

Ideally, everyone closely involved should be present. Therefore, there may be people from within an organisation, and 'outsiders', at the debrief. There must be no 'observers' at a debrief. Nor should there be any senior executives to 'monitor' what is said.

People should not be expected to return to work immediately after a debrief.

A problem arises if some people have physical injuries that prevent them attending the debriefing session. They may still be hospitalised, so that a compromise has to be sought. The debriefing needs to be arranged to allow the maximum number of people to attend. Those who cannot attend because they are too ill, or for other personal reasons, need to be carefully monitored without that monitoring becoming intrusive, counterproductive or offensive.

What time has to be set aside for the debriefing?

An average time for a debriefing session is thought to be around three and a half hours. It may be that a session can be wrapped up quickly in a little over one hour. That does not necessarily make it a bad debriefing. The largest sections of time during the debriefing should be in establishing the facts of the incident (at least one third of the time) and assessing people's feelings about the incident (also at least one third of the time – possibly longer).

What happens after the debriefing?

Refreshments should be available and time allowed for people to approach the debriefer independently. There should also be plenty of time to gather information about the next stage in the incident – which might be a court case or an inquest. Lastly, there should be details of where the family and supporters of those involved may seek assistance themselves.

Debriefing can be used for those who have experienced one traumatic incident, or for those who have endured more than one incident. Clearly, the more incidents that an individual has experienced, the more complex the debriefing is likely to become, and the greater the risk of suffering from PTSD, or Complex PTSD.

Debriefing must never be viewed as an antidote to PTSD. It is not a magical cure that inoculates victims from the effects of trauma. It is simply a first-aid remedy that will, if carried out properly and sympathetically, reduce the risks of victims being diagnosed as suffering from PTSD.

The debriefing should *not* be seen as the end of the matter. It is not even the beginning of the end. It is simply the end of the beginning.

Debriefing models

Although every debriefing session is slightly different, and those running the sessions will develop the debriefing according to what those present appear to require, there are several generally accepted models for debriefing: the Mitchell model, the Dyregrov model and a three-stage revised model adapted by such debriefers as Parkinson and others (Parkinson 1997).

My own preference is for an eclectic approach to debriefing as illustrated in the Emotional Decompression model. The rigidity of sticking to one model often suffocates the effectiveness of the debriefing.

The four major models – in a simple format – are set out in some detail here for your interest and for comparison. It can be seen that debriefing models generally come in five, six or seven stages. The language used within each model tends to differ subtly and only slightly, but there are some significant differences which will be explored and compared later in this text. Perhaps the best way to compare these models is simply to lay them side by side.

The Mitchell debriefing (see Table 2.2)

Mitchell's Critical Incident Stress Debriefing (CISD) model was first presented officially in 1983 and was based on some of Mitchell's earlier work (Mitchell and Everly 2001). Originally, it had only six phases but in 1984 it was modified slightly and made a seven-phase model. CISD was originally aimed at emergency service workers and those working in the casualty departments of hospitals. There were various attempts at debriefing prior to the introduction of the 1983 model, but there is a degree of vagueness as to the quality and content of those interventions.

The Dyregrov debriefing (see Table 2.3)

Atle Dyregrov is the director of the Center of Crisis Psychology in Bergen, Norway. Much of his work has been focused on children and families. His debriefing model is a little more detailed than Mitchell's, and perhaps shows his different psychological background.

The three-stage revised debriefing (after Parkinson) (see Table 2.4)

Frank Parkinson worked for many years as an army chaplain and developed his own three-stage model of debriefing based upon his own experiences of dealing with soldiers who were traumatised by events in the Gulf War. The model, which is often referred to as 'the three Fs', is a slight variation again. It is possibly the most widely used model within the UK, but that may be changing as practitioners explore 'best practice' and realise that Parkinson's model can be a little superficial in certain areas.

Emotional Decompression model (after Kinchin) (see Table 2.5)

David Kinchin is a retired police officer from the Thames Valley police service. He actually suffered from PTSD which (as far as he knows) makes him unique among those whose work is being presented here.

Table 2.2 Model: The Mitchell debriefing

1.	Introduction and rules	
2.	Facts	What happened?
		What did you do?
		How did others treat you?
		How did the incident end?
3	Thoughts	What did you think?
		What did you do?
		How did you treat others?
		How did the incident end?
4.	Reactions	How did you feel in the beginning, and later?
		What was the worst thing about it for you?
		How do you feel now?
5.	Symptoms	What physical and emotional reactions did you experience:
		(i) at the time?
		(ii) later?
6.	Teaching	Debriefer emphasises the normality of their reactions
		Debriefer prepares the debriefees for possible future reactions
7.	Re-entry	What support is needed?
		What support is available?
		Any questions? Issue information and leaflets
		Remain available when debriefing is over
		Follow-up essential; referral as necessary

Time: minimum of two hours.

Table 2.3 Model: The Dyregrov debriefing

1.	Introduction and rules	
2.	Expectations and facts	What happened? What did you expect? How did others treat you? How did the incident end?
3.	Thoughts and sensory impressions	What did you think in the beginning and later? What did you do, and why? What sights, sounds, smells, tastes, touch sensations did you experience?
4.	Emotional reactions	How did you feel at the beginning and later? What was the worst thing about it for you? How do you feel now?
5.	Normalisation	Debriefer reassures debriefees of the normality of their reactions Debriefer explains possible reactions
6.	Future planning and coping	What help do you (or your family) need? What support do you (or your family) need? What have you learned?
7.	Disengagement	Any questions? Issue information, leaflets Follow-up and referral as necessary Debriefer remains behind after session

Time: minimum of three hours.

Table 2.4 Model: The three-stage revised debriefing

Stage	Name	Content
Introduction		
Stage 1	The Facts	What was happening *before* the incident?
		What happened *during* the incident?
		What happened *after* the incident?
Stage 2	The Feelings	Sensory impressions
		Sights, sounds, smells, touch, taste
	Emotions	What feelings and emotions were generated?
	Reactions	What physical reactions?
		What feelings and reactions are present now?
		Any positive reactions?
		Lessons learned?
Stage 3	The Future	Normalisation
		Debriefer explains all reactions are normal
		Gives information about possible reactions
		Support: personal, group, organisational, external
		The aftermath: court cases, inquests, inquiries, funerals
Endings	Final Statements	Referrals
		Refreshments

Time: minimum of three hours.

Adapted from Parkinson 1997

Table 2.5 Model: Emotional Decompression

Stage	Name	Content
Introduction	Diving in	Debriefers introduce themselves Debriefers explain the aim and purpose Debriefers explain the rules and agree them with debriefees
Stage 1	Deep water	What was happening *before* the incident? What happened *during* the incident? What happened *after* the incident?
Stage 2	Middle water	What physical reactions were experienced? What feelings and reactions are present now? Any positive reactions? Lessons learned? Sensory impressions What feelings and emotions were generated?
Stage 3	Breaking the surface	Debriefer explains all reactions are normal Debriefer gives information about possible future reactions Coping. Strategies to watch out for snakes and ladders model of recovery explained Support: personal, group, organisational, external The aftermath. Court cases, inquests, inquiries, funerals
Endings	Treading water	Final statements Referrals? Further information Refreshments

Time: minimum of one and a half hours.

Debriefing for emergency services/armed forces (Kinchin 2004)

Kinchin's model is based upon the practical experience of working with the emergency services and listening to their particular needs and requirements. Much of the work for this model was devised while working with officers from the North Wales police service, and is intended for practitioners working in pairs.

Many debriefers will be aware of these different models. This isn't intended to be a competition to find the best, or the cheapest to administer, or the quickest. The aim of this text continues to be an awareness of all the available models so that practitioners may pick the best to suit their needs.

Other lesser known models of debriefing
Bohl's model

In Bohl's programme for debriefing, she suggests that the first intervention takes place as soon after the critical incident as possible (Bohl 1995). A first intervention may involve a single person 'defusing' within 24 hours, followed later by a second one-to-one, with a follow-up group debriefing taking place within one week to encourage group cohesion and bonding. This model is primarily for law enforcement officers but could be modified for other groups.

The real difference with the Bohl model is that it makes no real distinction between the cognitive and the emotional phases of the debrief. If an officer starts to explain their emotional feelings during the fact phase or the cognitive phase of the debrief, then Bohl contests there is little point in stopping them, stalling them until a little later on. On reflection, however, other models allow for flexibility and common sense in the structuring of debriefings, and everybody understands the need to respond empathetically towards the clients who are being debriefed.

The Bohl model contains an additional phase, not found in any other model, of 'unfinished business'. Clients are asked: 'What in the present situation reminds you of past experiences?' If ever there was a question which might open a whole new can of worms, it is that! To give her credit, Bohl maintains that this question came about following her observations of debriefs. Current traumas often act as a catalyst for the recall of previous experiences, and this question gives an opening for officers who wish to talk about how this event might compare with a previous one.

The dealing with 'unfinished business' from previous events could actually hijack the debrief and make it totally pointless for other people in the group. The counter view is that others may actually learn from this sharing of experiences. I suggest that dealing with 'unfinished business' is not the task of a peer debriefer but may be appropriate for a fully trained counsellor to explore at a later date on a one-to-one level. So the question might be: 'Is there anything in the present situation that reminds you of past experiences, that you think means you need to be referred…?'

Raphael's model

Beverley Raphael's model (1986) for psychological debriefing is not as prescriptive as those of Mitchell and Dyregrov. She begins the debriefing with what happened before the incident and asks the participants about the level of training or preparation they received before the traumatic experience took place. Raphael asks questions such as 'Was your life threatened?' or 'Did you lose anyone close to you?' Although this kind of information may emerge from other types of debriefing, Raphael is much more direct with her questioning and also tries to look at the positive as well as the negative side of things. Questions such as 'Did you feel good about anything that you did?' help to promote positive angles to the trauma. The debriefing focuses on what has been learned from the experience and how this can help participants in the future.

FBI Critical Incident Stress Management Programme

This programme has been organised with the explicit use of peer support in mind. Team members are drawn from staff, FBI chaplains and mental health professionals. They appear to use a standard CISD debriefing model along the lines suggested by Mitchell. The debriefing is then followed up with one-to-one peer support. The support from a fellow agent, who has 'been there', is found to give an enhanced credibility to the whole programme.

The unique feature of the FBI Critical Incident Stress Management Program (McNally and Solomon 1999) is a post critical incident seminar approximately four days after the event. This seminar may include 15–25 individuals who will meet in a safe place, in a retreat-like environment, where they can access clinicians who specialise in traumatic stress. The FBI also endorses a therapeutic technique known as 'eye movement desensitisation and reprocessing' (EMDR), which is one of only two therapeutic techniques recognised in the UK for treating PTSD (the other being cognitive behavioural therapy).

Integrative debriefing

Regehr and Bober (2004) have proposed a debriefing protocol that purportedly builds on the strength of earlier models while trying to modify some elements which they felt were counterproductive. The model divides into six phases:

1. Introduction – A discussion as to the purpose of the meeting.

2. Shared understanding – A sharing of the participants' understanding of exactly what took place.

3. Impact of experience – The effects of the incident are discussed. Special attention is placed on the impact on relationships with family and friends, something glossed over by other more traditional debriefings.

4. Strategies for coping – A sharing of the group's coping strategies.

5. Mobilising social supports – This capitalises on the camaraderie of the debriefing to promote ongoing support for the group. However, in my view, few things promote cynicism more than trying to force-feed a bogus sense of unity within a group, so care is necessary.

6. Wrap-up – The participants are *thanked* for coming and for their willingness to engage and share. Strengths are reinforced and

opportunities for some sort of follow-up are provided. The most distressed are encouraged to access additional mental health care.

Armstrong's model

This model of debriefing claims to be designed as a Multiple Stressor Debriefing (MSD) for use with the emergency services. Armstrong, O'Callaghan and Marmar (1991) claim to have modified the Mitchell defusing model to address the problem of disaster workers involved in having multiple contacts with victims, long hours and a poor working environment. The main difference between this model and others is the emphasis on past reactions to stressors and coping styles.

Line-of-duty Death Debriefing

Perhaps the ultimate stressor for anyone is the death of a colleague, particularly if it has been a close relationship. Line-of-duty Death Debriefing (LODD) (Mitchell and Levenson 2006) is modified into a five-phased protocol that is actually conducted on the day of the death and frequently lasts between 30 and 45 minutes. Perhaps it is more in line with what others refer to as defusing, rather than debriefing.

The five phases of the LODD are:

1. Introduction – As everyone to an extent knows everyone else already, introductions can be kept to a minimum, if required at all.

2. Fact phase – Any missing or ambiguous information is always more stressful than the grimmest of known facts. Therefore, officers are asked to describe briefly what happened so that others can glean the full facts of the incident.

3. Reaction phase – Participants are asked the question, 'What are you having the most difficulty with right now?' Most officers are still emotionally raw at this early stage so a full debriefing model would not work effectively.

4. Teaching phase – This is used to prepare officers for the funeral and to encourage them to do things that will help them take care of themselves as they cope with this loss.

5. Re-entry phase – This is generally a question and answer session, and a summarising of the full process of dealing with death.

In this model, a full seven-phase CISD is usually offered three to seven days later as a follow-up to this introduction, which is a more streamlined five-stage process on the day of the death.

This model shows just how easy it is to become muddled about the terms 'debriefing' and 'defusing', and how confused different organisations can become if they do not stick to an established strategy for assisting staff who have been traumatised.

Salutogenic debriefings

One group of commentators on the subject of psychological debriefing, Violanti, Paton and Dunning (2000), advocate a radical shift in the theory and its practice. Their primary criticism of the traditional debriefing is that it allows employers to discharge their obligation to the emotionally wounded cheaply. They are worried that the quick-fix, one-size-fits-all package of therapeutic intervention is not the best way forward. These authors propose an alternative 'salutogenic debriefing' model that views any critical incident as an opportunity for personal growth. This is an avoidance of the 'Clarence the angel' technique or learned helplessness (from the film *It's a Wonderful Life*), which these commentators feel is going too far. I am not totally sure where Violanti *et al.* are going with this suggestion as all debriefings make an attempt to reduce hopelessness and helplessness and foster adaptive coping. Violanti *et al.* feel we are going too far. Debriefing, like all successful treatments, must be a living and evolving organism while practitioners seek 'best practice' at all times. Table 2.6 shows a comparison of debriefing models that may assist best practice.

Table 2.6 Comparison of stages in four models of debriefing

Mitchell	Dyregrov	Raphael	Armstrong
Introduction and rules	Introduction and rules	Introduction and rules	Introduction and rules
Facts	Expectations and facts	Initiation into disaster	Identification of events that are most troubling
Thoughts	Thoughts and decisions	Experience of disaster	
Reactions	Sensory impressions	Negative/positive aspects and feelings	Feelings and reactions to difficult events
Symptoms	Emotional reactions	Relationships with others	Coping strategies past and present
Teaching	Normalisation	Feelings of victims	
Re-entry	Future planning and coping		Termination
	Disengagement	Disengagement Review and close	Focus on leaving the disaster and returning home

Adapted from Tehrani 2004

The view today

During the early stages of the twenty-first century, a 'myth' was established that early intervention was of little or no benefit and may actually harm people. This was in sharp contrast to the needs expressed by traumatised people. Although this myth with its resulting debate may help us to critically review the early responses which help people following traumatic events, there is also a grave danger of 'throwing the baby out with the bath water' (Dyregrov 2003).

Early intervention needs to be well organised and structured. It needs to contain more than just provision of comfort and a chance to come together. The services provided for the traumatised must go beyond the provision of debriefing, and should encompass other areas of support appropriate to the needs of the individual client.

We have advanced much more in the field of trauma therapy in recent years than we have done in areas of early intervention. There was a period when too many people, without proper training, were rushing in to do more or less helpful interventions, calling these interventions 'debriefing'. These 'ambulance chasers' gave the whole process a bad name, but now the pendulum has swung the other way and people are joining the bandwagon of suggesting that we wait with any form of intervention. This debate does have one major consequence. It has led to a more flexible view of early intervention and driven away some of the hard and fast rules which were previously, and erroneously, applied to all situations.

The biology of PTSD – dual attention theory

One of the newer theories about trauma is Brewin's (2001) dual attention theory which has been supplemented by Turnbull (2003). It is postulated that there are two different memory systems, one called the verbally accessible memory (VAM) and the other situational, or sensory accessible memory (SAM). While the first system uses the verbal mode and contains easily accessible memory information that can be communicated to others through language and speech, the SAM system contains personal, perception-based information dependent upon the different sensory channels. Information is not verbally encoded and is harder to communicate to others. The 'bridge' joining the two memories is the hippocampus which acts like a fuse. This fuse may be damaged or destroyed during a traumatic event and so prevent the VAM and SAM memory systems sharing information.

Flashbacks are one way of gradually allowing SAM memories into the VAM system and then integrating them into the memories of past and present. As the hippocampus recovers, so the number and intensity of flashbacks will decrease.

It is suggested that while these hippocampus 'bridges' are destroyed and flashbacks are at their height, debriefing is ineffective and may even be harmful as a re-exposure to the trauma. Waiting for the regeneration of the hippocampus may take as long as a month. Therefore, it may be logical and sensible to delay debriefing by as much as one month in some cases.

The eclectic approach to early intervention

Now the dust is settling following the debate which has developed the myth of bad early intervention, it is time to move forward and provide best practice for those in need of support. Best practice should include good quality early intervention.

The term 'debriefing' has been damaged by this debate so it has been suggested that it should be replaced (Raphael and Wilson 2000). The umbrella term 'early intervention' is now more readily used, but other phrases are starting to appear in texts. My own feeling is that the term 'Emotional Decompression' is appropriate, and to many the word 'decompression' suggests a staged approach to a recovery situation.

There is also a need for a flexible approach with a structure that allows for adaptation to individual needs rather than being prescriptive and rigid (Tehrani 2002). Much of the myth about debriefing came about because it was researched in isolation. Indeed, in some cases it was used as a therapy in isolation. Early interventions should not be used in isolation but must form part of a carefully managed care package for those who are traumatised. Within the framework of the post-trauma care package, there is a most definite need for early interventions along the lines of those commonly called debriefing.

The approach to debriefing/early intervention/emotional decompression (whatever *you* wish to call it) should be an eclectic one. In the same way that trauma counsellors have access to a number of different and complementary counselling theories, so those who practise early intervention should work in much the same way.

The strict rules about the timing of any intervention should be disregarded. There is plenty of anecdotal evidence to suggest that a carefully tailored debriefing can be offered to a client two days, two weeks, two months or even two years after the initial trauma. Indeed, it is logical if the dual attention theory is applied that a significant number of debriefings may take place around one month after the trauma.

During training sessions for debriefers, which I have facilitated, it has become clear that far too many experienced debriefers have become frustrated by the selfsame rules with which they were originally happy to comply. At the end of the course, delegates have been refreshed by the knowledge that they can (if they wish) sit clients around a table to debrief them. They can delay a debriefing by three or four days in order to get the full shift of officers together in one place at one time. They can use the Mitchell model for one debriefing and then shift to another model, which they feel is more appropriate, for another debriefing. Indeed, they can take the elements from all the available debriefing models and compose their own model with which they are confident and comfortable. The object is to offer best practice to the clients, not pay homage to a particular model of treatment.

Looking at the time taken to complete a debriefing session, this can vary from a little over an hour to as much as four hours' duration. Debriefing a small group of well-trained emergency service staff may only take 60 minutes. Debriefing one rape victim may take all day.

Legal issues in peer support and critical incident services

Currently in the UK, there is no specific code of ethics for debriefers. It is simply assumed that many of those who undertake to run debriefing sessions are already members of counselling organisations and so will abide by one of those associations' code of ethics. This is most likely to be the British Association of Counsellors and Psychologists (BACP) or the Association of Christian Counsellors (ACC). Both have very comprehensive codes of ethics which are available from their head offices or via their websites.

However, many peer debriefers are not actually members of BACP or ACC and so cannot be encouraged to comply with these codes. 'Good practice' and common sense require that some guidelines be applied to all defusing and debriefing sessions. Those who participate in such sessions have expectations of the practitioners offering these services, and need to have some kind of safeguard.

One of the main legal issues involves privileged communication and confidentiality. Under various laws in the UK and USA, patients are entitled to confidentiality when speaking to a doctor or other accredited clinician. This means that any investigation into the activities of anyone who has consulted these professionals in any way remains private and the patient's records are regarded as strictly confidential. The exception is when the patient authorises the release of the information.

Peer debriefers do not have this luxury, however, and cannot hide behind any law which protects them from releasing information which has been presented to them in any defusing or debriefing scenario. The way most peer debriefers get around this perceived difficulty is to never keep written records of the debriefing other than the time, date and register of those who were present.

Another legal issue arises from the possibility that participants' views of the trauma will change after their debriefing – this is inevitable. Therefore, it is strongly advised that all official records, such as witness statements, should be provided to the appropriate authorities *before* any debriefing takes place. This removes the possibility of the suggestion being made in a court of law that a participant's view of the trauma has been contaminated by the views of others during the debriefing process.

Debriefers themselves also need some protection in law. Participants may be strongly affected by the debriefing process – perhaps complaining that the debriefing made them worse instead of better. Debriefers need to be insured against any such claims of negligence on their part. This insurance can be obtained through the usual channels of counselling insurance so long as it is clearly stated that the person is acting in the role of a debriefer. In disciplined services such as the police and the armed forces, the fact that a debriefer has attended all the necessary training and is acting under the orders of a senior officer may be sufficient. The debriefer is then seen to be executing a duty which has been ordered.

Bibliography

Armstrong, K., O'Callaghan, W. and Marmar, C.R. (1991) 'Debriefing Red Cross disaster personnel: the multiple stressor debriefing model.' *Journal of Traumatic Stress 4*, 4, 581–593.

Bohl, N. (1995) 'Professionally Administered Critical Incident Debriefing for Police Officers.' In M. Kunke and E. Scrivner (eds) *Police Psychology in the 21st Century.* Hillsdale, NJ: Erlbaum.

Brewin, C.R. (2001) 'A cognitive neuroscience account of post-traumatic stress disorder and its treatment.' *Behaviour Research Therapy 39*, 373–393.

Dyregrov, A. (2003) *Psychological Debriefing: A Leader's Guide to Small Group Crisis Intervention.* Ellicott City: Chevron.

Kinchin, D. (2004) *Post Traumatic Stress Disorder: The Invisible Injury.* Oxon: Success Unlimited.

McNally, V. and Solomon, R. (1999) 'The FBI's critical incident stress management program.' *FBI Law Enforcement Bulletin*, February, 20–26.

Mitchell, J. and Everly, G.S. (2001) *Critical Incident Stress Debriefing.* Ellicott City: Chevron.

Mitchell, J. and Levenson, R.L. (2006) 'Some thoughts on providing effective mental health care for police departments after line-of-duty deaths.' *International Journal of Emergency Mental Health 8*, 1, 1–14.

Parkinson, F. (1997) *Critical Incident Debriefing: Understanding and Dealing with Trauma.* London: Souvenir Press.

Raphael, B. (1986) *When Disaster Strikes: A Handbook for Caring Professions.* London: Hutchinson.

Raphael, B. and Wilson, J. (2000) *Psychological Debriefing: Theory, Practice and Evidence.* Cambridge: Cambridge University Press.

Regehr, C. and Bober, T. (2004) *In the Line of Fire: Trauma in the Emergency Services.* New York: Oxford University Press.

Tehrani, N. (2002) *Workplace Trauma: Concepts, Assessment and Interventions.* New York: Brunner-Routledge.

Tehrani, N. (2004) *Workplace Trauma: Concepts, Assessment and Interventions.* Second edition. New York: Brunner-Routledge.

Turnbull, G. (2003) Unpublished notes of presentation given to the Sunderland Counselling Service, 18 September.

Violanti, J., Paton, D. and Dunning, C. (eds) (2000) *Post Traumatic Stress Intervention: Challenges, Issues and Perspectives.* Springfield: Charles C. Thomas.

CHAPTER THREE

Emotional Decompression

The previous chapter dealt with the various models of psychological debriefing. It is the task of this chapter to explain in detail what goes on during a debriefing. To do that, we are going to explore the model of Emotional Decompression, but fans of other debriefing models need not be disheartened because there is so much overlap from model to model that it is easy to work out how other models might progress simply by studying this model.

Preparation

Even before we get to the stage where debriefers introduce themselves to the participants, there is some preparation that is necessary. Where is the debriefing to be held? It needs to be in a room which can guarantee quietness and no interruptions. Also, the room must not be overlooked by others – participants may become distressed during the process of debriefing and they will not want outsiders to witness this distress through the windows of an office or boardroom.

There needs to be easy and convenient access to toilet facilities. Facilities for offering tea, coffee and soft drinks must also be available. It would be best to be able to offer people decaffeinated drinks as the last thing their bodies will need is a stimulant such as caffeine.

Think about how the furniture might be arranged in the room – what are the seats like? Participants want to be able to be comfortable for up to three hours so they will not appreciate unpadded seats. Debriefers need to decide how the seats are to be arranged (see Figures 3.1–3.4). Some sort of circle is often the preferred choice of seasoned

Figure 3.1: The debriefing process – small debriefing room arrangement

Figure 3.2: The debriefing process – small debriefing room arrangement with table

Figure 3.3: The debriefing process – large debriefing room arrangement

Figure 3.4: The debriefing process – classroom debriefing room arrangement

debriefers, while others prefer to be gathered around a table in the middle of the room. Although there is no research that stipulates how the seating should be arranged for a debriefing, there is plenty of anecdotal evidence to suggest that participants like to be seated in such a way that they can see everyone else. Therefore, a classroom seating arrangement is not recommended.

Debriefers need to decide where they are gong to sit. If there are two or more debriefers present in the room, then it is best to sit opposite each other so that each debriefer has a good view of part of the group. If debriefers sit beside each other, it creates an 'us and them' situation and debriefers are unable to make eye contact with each other. Plan your seating arrangement to best suit your style of debriefing.

Another piece of preparation is to decide how much you need to know about the situation that you are going to debrief. There are two schools of thought here. Parkinson's (1997) view is that 'It is essential that a debriefer does not go into a debriefing knowing nothing about the incident – to visit the scene may also be very useful' (p. 134). However, some debriefers still prefer to go into the debriefing 'cold' without any knowledge of the event that has required the debrief. This way, they are not prejudiced either one way or the other about the event. Occasionally, though, it can be hugely disadvantageous to go into a debrief 'blind' in this way. Many seasoned debriefers like to be made aware of the facts of the event before the debriefing starts. This enables any element of shock, distaste or other raw emotion to be overcome before the debriefing starts. The last thing any debriefing wants is for those leading it to become overwhelmed by their own emotions at what they are hearing for the first time.

Often, the facts of the debrief are already known as the circumstances of the event may have featured in press coverage or internal publications within the organisation.

Diving in: Introductions

With all the preparation completed, the debrief is now ready for the introductory stage of the process. Everyone should introduce themselves to the group and state very briefly how they were linked to the event. These opening few words are very important. The debriefer may well pick up clues as to how people are feeling about the event simply by listening to their voices as they introduce themselves and by observing the participants' body language as the spotlight moves around the group in turn.

The debriefer(s) play the major role in this stage of the proceedings. It is important that rules are established. Mobiles, pagers and radios need to be turned off completely. Just one person answering a phone call or a radio message can completely destroy the mood of the debriefing. This is a golden rule.

There should be no outsiders with the group. Sometimes in emergency service organisations a senior officer may feel the urge to sit in on the group and observe what is going on. In industry, it may be that a senior executive or welfare officer may want to observe what takes place. All such intruders should be barred from the debriefing. They can have operational debriefs at a later date. This psychological debriefing is for the benefit of staff, not for the scrutiny of senior members of staff – no exceptions.

It is important that confidentiality is mentioned. The debriefing process should be regarded as a confidential experience during which there is no note-taking. Participants need to feel that this confidentiality is adhered to completely. The task of the debriefer is to assure all present that what they say will be kept confidential. However, if participants start to disclose something which may make them liable to prosecution for a criminal offence, then they should be warned immediately that the confidentiality clause may be broken. Debriefings are not like confessionals in church.

Nor are debriefings like consultations with a family doctor. A debriefing is often run by peers for the benefit of their workmates and colleagues. Therefore, there is no protection in law such as the Hippocratic Oath which covers doctors. If a debriefer feels that a participant of the debriefing is about to disclose something which makes them liable to prosecution, then they should be stopped immediately and the possible repercussions of their disclosure explained to them.

For example, a factory worker may say that they were in the boss's office at the time of the accident because they were going to have a sneaky look at some confidential documents concerning the Christmas party – nothing really criminal about that so it can be kept confidential. However, if the same worker was in the boss's office because they were altering the overtime figures on the computer, then they had actually committed a criminal offence and it is not the responsibility of the debriefer to protect them from the consequences of such actions.

No notes are taken at a peer debriefing session. The only record made is of who attended the session. However, if a therapist is running the debriefing for a client who is likely to remain a client for further therapeutic sessions, then it seems reasonable that limited clinical notes might be made by the debriefer. This is one of several instances where *peer debriefing* may differ from a debriefing undertaken by a counsellor or psychotherapist.

Linked to the topic of confidentiality, participants will be asked to decide as a group whether or not they feel it is appropriate to discuss the debriefing in detail with their loved ones. If a person has experienced a severe trauma, then a wife, husband or other partner will naturally want to support their partner as much as possible. Part of that support will mean the sharing of actions and feelings associated with the traumatic event. If a person thinks their loved one is holding back and not telling the full story, that can sometimes test a relationship at a time when it may already be stressed by events. It is not the task of a debriefing to come between life partners in any way, so often groups will agree among themselves that it is okay to tell their partners, in some detail, about the debriefing. It is possible for life partners to share such information without the confidentiality of individuals being compromised in any way. This should be discussed by the group before the debriefing gets under way.

It must be made clear, by the actions and disposition of the debriefer(s), that the rules need to be agreed or negotiated before the debriefing itself commences. The group may want specific rules about having comfort breaks, or whether or not to allow someone to rejoin the group if they walk out for some reason.

The debriefing is neither an investigation nor a forum for complaints, although sometimes criticism of the system or of individuals will be voiced.

Finally, this introductory stage of the debriefing should be used to remind participants that they may actually feel slightly worse after the debriefing than they do immediately before it. This is normal and quite natural. The debriefing is going to put them in touch with their emotions at the time when they faced a very traumatic situation. It is inevitable that such a journey is going to reawaken some feelings and worries. However, this should very soon pass.

The aim of the psychological debriefing is 'to clarify the event and make sense of what participants recall – it is to share your recollections with others' (Kinchin 2004). Participants need to know that 'they do not have to react to be normal, but that it is normal to react' (p. 132).

Stage 1 – Deep water: Facts

This stage is very important in finding out what happened. The debriefer will try and put together the story, with the aid of all the participants, so that a full picture of the event can be established. This fact-finding mission will start with what people were doing immediately before they became aware of the event. It is important that the fact-finding starts with the normal events before the trauma started – this gives a base upon which the trauma story can be built.

This stage tests the active listening skills of the debriefer(s) as the story is teased out of the participants step-by-step. There is no need to rush things as this stage sets the tone for the whole debriefing. Participants will be watching the debriefers to see how they react to the story as it unfolds. This information exchange is a two-way street in that respect. Debriefers need to be aware of their own body language as they listen to the story that is told to them. Non-verbal communication skills are as important as listening skills in this instance, and debriefers need to be aware of the fundamental active listening skills which all trained counsellors have as a matter of basic training. It is interesting that a minority of accredited counsellors and psychotherapists are very much against peer debriefing because they have the ill-conceived idea that active listening skills cannot be learned by people in other professions. They tend to forget that many other professions require the use of active listening skills but those skills may not be known by the terms which are familiar to counsellors.

Debriefers must be aware of the effects of any gestures they may use (perhaps out of habit) and should also learn that silence can be a very effective listening skill in a debriefing situation. Even the way a debriefer might dress and present themselves to the group says something about that debriefer.

Typical listening skills that might be used during a debriefing are paraphrasing, reflecting, summarising, asking open questions, empathy, challenging, immediacy and self-disclosure (Hough 1998). Questions which might be asked at this stage of the debriefing might include:

- What did you think would happen?
- What did happen?
- What did you expect?
- What did you actually do?
- How were you prepared?
- What could have happened?

The core conditions for counselling suggested as essential by the therapist Carl Rogers (Hough 1998) can be applied to psychological debriefing in much the same way. The three conditions of empathy, unconditional positive regard (UPR) and congruence or genuineness should apply to all debriefing scenarios.

- Empathy – In this instance, empathy describes the debriefer's ability to understand the participants at a deep level. This is something which is much easier said than done since it involves an awareness of what it is the client is actually experiencing. Experience has shown that peer debriefers are much more easily able to adhere to this core condition than professional debriefers who are brought into the organisation specifically for the debriefing process. Empathy is not the same thing as sympathy.

- UPR – The need for positive regard is present in all humans and readers will be aware that young children will do almost anything in order to achieve some positive regard. Rogers believed that counsellors (debriefers) should convey UPR or warmth towards clients if they are to feel understood and accepted. This means that clients are valued and accepted without any conditions attached, even when they may experience themselves as negative, frightened or unworthy.

- Congruence or genuineness – This quality is one of sincerity, authenticity and honesty within the counselling (debriefing) relationship. In order to be congruent with the participants of a debriefing, the debriefers need to be themselves, without any pretence or façade. Of course this means that debriefers need to know themselves first. An important aspect of genuineness is that it acts as a model for the participants who may find it difficult to be open and genuine themselves. Another term used by some commentators is 'being real'.

Stage 2 – Middle water: Feelings

Now we start to explore how participants felt during the traumatic event. These feelings can be explored in much the same way as the facts in the previous stage of the debriefing. However, sticking to a logical progression of feelings is sometimes not as easy as it sounds.

Participants are asked to explore their sensory impressions of the event. What were their senses telling them? Sights, sounds, touch, taste and smell may all be important in describing the feelings which were experienced. It is difficult to single out one sense over the others because all traumatic events are different, but experience and anecdotal evidence suggest that smell can play a very important part in the recall of events during a trauma. Very often that same smell can act as a trigger to remind participants of the trauma, and that trigger can still operate many years after the trauma has passed (something the debriefer can share with the participants while debriefing).

It is important to try and involve everyone in this phase of the debriefing, while at the same time acknowledging that nobody is forced to participate.

The debriefer needs to pay particular attention to individuals who might be exhibiting any difficulties in sharing their feelings because they are too distressed.

This stage may be brought to a useful conclusion by asking participants how they felt:

- at home, after the event
- that night
- right now!

It can be seen in Figure 3.5 showing the flow of a debriefing that the path of the debrief dips into the stack of emotions and then smoothly comes out as the emotions themselves begin to 'normalise'.

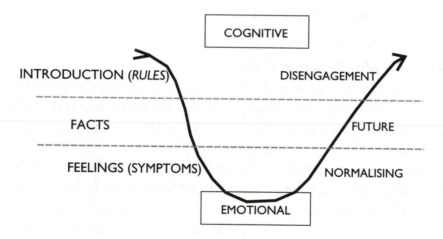

Figure 3.5: The debriefing process (adapted from Mitchell and Everly 2001)

While looking at emotions and feelings, it is useful to see if there are any positive reactions within the group, or any useful lessons which have been learned.

Normalising

Coming to the end of this stage of the debriefing, it is the responsibility of the debriefer(s) to normalise the feelings which have been brought to the group. It needs to be stressed that the feelings are normal – it is the event which was abnormal and difficult to cope with. Not everyone will react in the same way. It is vitally important to normalise any actions and reactions which might have taken place. This stage may include a little bit of teaching about coping mechanisms, such as the use of black humour or the ability some people have to almost shut down emotionally and allow their training to take over.

Stage 3 – Breaking the surface: Future

This is very much a teaching phase for the debriefer to take charge of the process once again. Participants will need to be made aware of any support networks which already exist and which they may make use of. It is not just about the participants: others need to be aware of the impact the traumatic event has had. It is the task of all participants to engage with other people and tell them of the event (remembering the confidentiality of the group), and to teach others how to cope with such situations – indeed, to show that it is possible to cope with very traumatic situations.

The debriefer(s) now need to spend a little time teaching the group about Post-Traumatic Stress Disorder (PTSD). The group should be aware that they have all probably suffered an acute stress reaction but one that should be short-lived. If the symptoms of PTSD continue beyond a period of four weeks, then professional medical assistance should be sought. Teaching on PTSD is important so as to make participants aware of the types of things which may happen to them in the future, even the distant future. The snakes and ladders model of recovery from PTSD (Kinchin 1994) may be described to the group as a way of teaching them the significance of different traumatic symptoms.

Participants may have to attend court at some time in the future; this may be a Coroner's Court, Magistrate's Court, Crown Court or Civil Court. It may be that there are also funerals to attend. The group should be reminded that any or all these events may result in a renewal of symptoms which had diminished or ceased altogether. Participants may feel they have met a snake (see snakes and ladders model) which they may have difficulty in coping with. Forewarning of the impact of such an event can be invaluable.

Stage 4 – Treading water: Disengagement

It is important that the group is given time to ask any questions of the debriefers. It shouldn't all be one-way traffic and questions should be encouraged at this point. This is also the time to hand out any flyers with contact details of any caring professionals locally who could be contacted on a confidential basis.

Make sure that there are plenty of leaflets and flyers for everyone. It is important that the information-giving stage of the debriefing is as professional as the rest of the process. Debriefers should be courteous enough to thank the participants for attending. It may be that they do not feel they have gained anything from the experience themselves, but the debriefer can assure them that the information they have provided to the group may have been invaluable to others in their attempts to piece together an order of events. The Robin Hood syndrome has come into play and the 'memory rich' have assisted the 'memory poor' by adding to the pooled memory of the group. This has been a group exercise, for the good of the individuals within the group, and it is almost impossible to measure just how useful and effective it has been.

Debriefing is not a 'stand-alone' process though, and should always be a part of a package which the debriefer(s) should be aware of and inform the participants about. There may be a counselling service which is on call to support participants after the debriefing. There may be a local doctor or psychotherapist who is able to see clients on a confidential basis. Participants must not be given the impression that once the debriefing is over the event is dealt with and everyone should move on and forget about it – for some that will not be possible.

Those who have been critical of psychological debriefing as a process are often critical because some poorly advised organisations have offered debriefing as a stand-alone support mechanism. This has given debriefing a bad press in the past. Participants of a debriefing have been left to flounder with nothing in the way of continued support and pastoral care. The debriefers have a duty to the group to be available once the debriefing has finished and to answer questions on a one-to-one basis from participants who did not wish to ask questions within the group situation.

At the end of any debriefing, the debriefers should linger. Soft drinks and hot drinks should be made available, and there should be no rush to vacate the room. Following a debriefing, participants may require time to compose themselves before they face the outside world again. In some organisations and particularly in the emergency services, consideration should be given to allowing participants the rest of the day off. This may be a controversial suggestion, and a costly one, but employees who have just been through a potentially emotional re-experiencing of a traumatic event should be offered the time and space to reconsider how they have coped with that event.

Employers have a duty of care to those who work for them. An employee who crashes a motor vehicle an hour after experiencing a psychological debriefing may be in a position to criticise their employer for forcing them back to work too quickly. A compensation claim may follow such a chain of events at the expense of the employer.

Supervision for the debriefer

The debriefing is concluded as far as the participants are concerned, but what about the debriefer(s)? Is it over for them? Counsellors are required to undergo sessions of professional supervision after delivering a set number of counselling sessions to clients. Currently, there is no legal requirement for debriefers to have such supervision, but it is my view that such supervision should be sought. Supervision is of benefit to debriefers for a number of reasons:

- Loss of confidence and 'burnout' are less likely when supervision is regular.
- It gives the debriefer a clearer picture of transference and counter-transference issues.
- It allows the debriefer to appraise the skills and approaches used with debriefing groups.

- It provides support, guidance and encouragement and a different perspective.

- It affords time for reflection and thought.

- It is rewarding for debriefers, both intellectually and emotionally.

- It serves to identify the debriefer's own needs for counselling support.

Supervision is not the same as counselling, and the relationship between the debriefer and their supervisor is quite different. The supervisor provides a listening ear to the debriefer, and a safeguard that the debriefer is delivering a quality debrief without risk of personal emotional injury.

Numbers to be debriefed

There has been anecdotal evidence of large group debriefings. It has been suggested that groups with as many as 200 participants have been debriefed in one session. Whatever it was that went on in such a group, it was not a psychological debriefing as has been described in this book. It was a token gesture.

Psychological debriefs can only be delivered effectively to small groups. The debriefing can be delivered to a single client – usually on a one-to-one footing. At the other end of the spectrum, a group debriefing involving two or even three debriefers can be delivered to as many as 18 or 20 clients. It is almost impossible to deliver a quality debriefing to any more than 20 people. Ideally, there should be no more than 12 participants in a peer debriefing session. Dyregrov (2003) suggests 8–12 as the optimum size for a group.

If there is a large group of participants requiring debriefing, then consideration should be given to dividing the group and offering more than one debriefing opportunity. How that is achieved is up to the organisation involved, but any division should be attempted with great care and consideration for those involved.

Duration of a debriefing

It is not possible to limit the time for a full debriefing to take place. There have been situations of one-to-one debriefings which have taken over three hours to complete, and there have been group debriefings which have been concluded within an hour and a half. The process should not be rushed (and should not have time restraints imposed upon it), but at the same time there is no merit to lingering unnecessarily over the process. Experience has shown that when debriefing becomes a standard practice within an organisation (such as a police force), then, as time goes by and staff become more familiar with the debriefing process, the process speeds up a little. An average time for a psychological debriefing process using the Emotional Decompression model, and delivering the debriefing to ten people, might be in the region of 80 minutes.

Time-frame for a debriefing

Originally, it was suggested that debriefings be conducted at least 48 hours after the event, but within a time period of 96 hours. For a while, these figures were tinkered around with and slight changes were made to them.

Brewin's dual attention theory (Brewin 2001) and our awareness of the biology of PTSD have now blown these early timings clean out of the water. It is still agreed that debriefings should take place at least 48 hours after the event – but today there is no final time limit within which a debriefing must be held. Experts are now aware that effective debriefings can be held one week, one month or even a year after the event.

On rare occasions, successful debriefings have been undertaken a number of years after the traumatic event, this debriefing being the first session in a series of therapeutic meetings with a client on a one-to-one basis.

The optimum time for a debriefing to take place following a trauma is, in the view of the author, one to two weeks. This time-frame gives participants time to overcome the initial traumatic shock, it leaves time for statements and official interviews to take place, and it allows time for the practicalities of the debriefing session to be organised (date, time and venue).

Parkinson (1997) has attemped to calculate some sort of timetable for the different parts of the debriefing process. This is rather difficult to do because each debriefing will be so very different but, if you look at the percentage of time that is spent on each stage of the debriefing, that may be of greater use (see Table 3.1).

Table 3.1 Psychological Debriefing – approximate percentage timings

Introduction – Diving in		12%
Stage 1 – Deep water	Facts	33%
Stage 2 – Middle water	Feelings	33%
Stage 3 – Breaking the surface	Future	15%
Stage 4 – Treading water	Disengagement	7%
	Total	100%

NB: These figures are based upon the work of Parkinson and the practical experiences of Kinchin.

The figures demonstrate that stages one and two of a debriefing are both important and time-consuming. The time is most definitely not divided equally among the stages, although each stage is important in its own right and no stage should ever be omitted for any reason.

The role of co-debriefers

A co-debriefer is someone who has been trained as a debriefer and who may be either learning from, or taking an active part in, the debriefing. At the beginning, it is logical for the debriefer to explain what part the co-debriefer is to play in the debriefing session. The co-debriefer introduces themselves, and then chooses one of the following options:

- to say nothing after the introductions and just support the debriefer by their presence

- to observe the reactions of the others and, should anyone leave, go with them to provide support and help
- to take an active, prearranged, part in the debriefing
- to join in as and when they feel it is appropriate, asking questions and making comments.

If the co-debriefer is to take an active part, then they should have a meeting with the debriefer beforehand and decide who will deal with which stages of the debriefing. It should always be clear who is leading the debriefing and who is playing the supporting role – this reassures the participants.

Debriefing as a reality

This book has gone to great lengths to include some information about as many different debriefing models as possible. Many of the models have been explained and the stages have been described. In reality, the debriefing will not flow in a precise and predictable way. The Emotional Decompression model uses an introduction followed by four definite stages. In reality, it may be that a 'live debriefing' moves from Stage 1 (Deep water or Facts) into Stage 2 (Middle water or Feelings) and then, because of new information which has been mentioned by one of the group, it may refer back to Stage 1 of the model again to clarify a situation. All these models should be viewed as fluid.

Debriefers themselves will claim to be debriefers using the Mitchell model, or the Parkinson model. In reality though, if you observe their work, it is often the case that they have picked out elements from a number of models and, if the truth be told, they are using a model which is unique to them. There may be as many debriefing models as there are debriefers. This should not be a problem so long as the debriefer is aware of each model and well aware of what they are doing. The aim is to seek 'best practice in debriefing', and that means each debriefer working in a professional way and to their personal strengths within the field of debriefing. Debriefers have to be comfortable with the model they are using and should not be forced into any one tight school of thought that will restrict the way in which they work.

This individualism should not come as a surprise to anyone who has worked in the field of counselling and psychotherapy. Counsellors switch from model to model as they continually assess the issues that their clients present to them. When dealing with real live human beings, it is essential to be able to maintain a level of flexibility in your work.

Taking charge

It is the debriefer's responsibility to take charge of the debriefing and ensure that it runs as planned and that its aims are achieved. Without careful preparation and planning, debriefing will not work effectively; this can lead to further problems, such as anger, confusion and disorientation in the participants of a debriefing, and even end as disillusionment with the process as well as loss of confidence and credibility in the debriefer.

When is it not advisable to conduct a debriefing?

Based on common sense and the issues which have been described earlier, it can be seen that it is sometimes not advisable to conduct a psychological debriefing. Such times may include when:

- strong conflicts existed in the group before the trauma
- very authoritative leaders are present in the group
- participants are too tired
- key people are missing
- a debrief has been offered but nobody appears to need it
- there is antagonism towards the debriefing itself
- (for individuals) regular flashback symptoms are being experienced.

If the timing of the event feels wrong to the debriefer, then perhaps the debriefing should be delayed or postponed until a more conducive time can be arranged. Once a debriefing has commenced, it should be seen through to its conclusion – no half measures are acceptable.

Group leaders – debriefers

Aveline (1993) suggests that the leader's task is to attend to the unattended details. By observing when the group 'nerve' is touched and by using past experience and knowledge, the leaders have to co-ordinate the discussion of important themes for the group, with flawless timing. The skills and aptitude of the group leaders (debriefers) dictate the fine-tuning of the group as to how briskly or slowly it moves, how deeply any theme is explored, when to change themes and when to move on to a new stage. This is of the utmost importance. Without the proper feel for a group, understanding of the process of debriefing and authority to steer it, the group is in danger of losing much of its potential benefit.

Positive outcomes from Psychological Debriefing

A number of good research studies have found positive outcomes from psychological debriefing. Similarly, there are reports of very negative situations resulting from groups of trauma victims who received no psychological debriefing after their trauma. It is appropriate to report some of these findings here as recorded by Saari (2005) in her book *A Bolt from the Blue.*

In 1987, the *Herald of Free Enterprise* sank in the English Channel and 196 of the 545 people who were on board died. Forty-two crew members were saved, of whom only two are reported to have returned to work at sea (Johnson 1993; Yule and Gold 1997).

In 1990, there was a fire on the car ferry *Scandinavian Star,* and 159 people lost their lives. A study found that, after three and a half years, 43 per cent of those saved had changed jobs and 39 per cent were experiencing serious problems at work or within their families (Elklit, Anderson and Aretander 1995). At the time of both these disasters, there was no preparedness to respond to the psychological needs of those who were involved in the disasters.

In 1992, Campbell studied the impact of psychological debriefing on the perceptions of FBI agents in processing traumatic events. The results of this study were statistically significant in five main areas:

1. Colleagues were no longer used as scapegoats.

2. Use of alcohol after shooting incidents decreased.

3. Attitudes to the job became more positive.

4. Severe counter-reactions decreased in other agents.

5. Isolation and loneliness reduced.

In 1994, Hanneman looked at the impact of psychological debriefing on volunteer firemen in Nova Scotia. She found effects in several areas:

1. Debriefing had a positive effect on the whole atmosphere of the department.

2. Debriefing had a positive effect on individuals' trauma processing.

3. The firemen acknowledged the importance of expressing feelings.

4. They acknowledged the importance of forming an overview of the whole incident.

5. They understood that they had done their best.

6. They became aware that other people had similar feelings.

7. The sense of cohesion and belonging increased.

Too often, researchers have been quick to analyse psychological debriefing purely on the basis of post-traumatic stress symptoms and scores on various questionnaires. It is also important to appreciate the 'feel-good' factor that may be generated by holding a debriefing and by organisations showing their staff that they really do care about them.

The benefits of an in-house peer debriefing programme are as follows:

1. The Emotional Decompression model of psychological debriefing is written specifically with the emergency services in mind. However, it is in user-friendly language and can be used by any organisation.

2. Debriefing is delivered by staff (in pairs) to other staff. The debriefers therefore already have 'credibility' established. An outsider coming into a debriefing session would have to prove themselves to the audience.

3. The programme has a strong emphasis on 'normalising' and 'teaching', which is not always the case in other models.

4. The tailor-made programme aims at 'best practice' in the field of psychological debriefing by exploring all the main debriefing styles as part of the training.

5. Staff are not asked to 'trust-a-stranger' because debriefers are likely to be already known to them. This actually cuts the time of a debrief, which is an added bonus.

6. Debriefing is not counselling. Therefore, it doesn't really make sense to insist that all debriefers should be trained counsellors. Staff are perfectly capable of learning the skills and knowledge required to deliver an effective debrief.

7. Debriefing staff frequently helps to build the team, and brings staff closer together as a unit.

8. Anecdotal evidence indicates that Emotional Decompression delivered by *peers* is very effective in keeping stress levels low.

9. Having the debriefs delivered by staff peers means the organisation still has a strong element of control over the process. The organisation would *not* have the same level of control if *outsiders* were brought in to undertake debriefs.

10. Average debrief times are under 90 minutes, compared with suggested timings of three hours using some other models of debriefing.

There is no time limit on when a debrief can be delivered. Some models stipulate that debriefs should be delivered 48–120 hours after the critical incident. Emotional Decompression can be delivered weeks after the event if required.

Bibliography

Aveline, M. (1993) 'Principles of leadership in brief training groups for mental health care professionals.' *Journal of Group Psychotherapy 43*, 107–129.

Brewin, C.R. (2001) 'A cognitive neuroscience account of post-traumatic stress disorder and its treatment.' *Behaviour Research Therapy 39*, 373–393.

Campbell, J. (1992) 'A comparative analysis of the effects of post shooting trauma on special agents of the FBI.' Unpublished dissertation. Michigan State University.

Dyregrov, A. (2003) *Psychological Debriefing: A Leader's Guide to Small Group Crisis Intervention.* Ellicott City: Chevron.

Elklit, A., Anderson, L.B. and Aretander, T. (1995) 'Scandinavian Star. Anden Del. En opfölgenende undersögelse af de fysiske, psykologiske og sociale eftervirkninger 3, 5 ar efter katastrofen.' *Psykologisk Skriftserie 20*, 2. Aarhus Universitet.

Hanneman, M. (1994) *Evaluation of Critical Incident Stress Debriefing as Perceived by Volunteer Firefighters in Nova Scotia.* Ann Arbor, MI: UMI Dissertation Service.

Hough, M. (1998) *Counselling Skills and Theory.* London: Hodder Arnold.

Johnson, A. (1993) 'Traumatic Stress Reactions in the Crew of the *Herald of Free Enterprise.*' In J. Wilson and B. Raphael (eds) *International Handbook of Traumatic Stress Syndromes.* New York: Plenum Press.

Kinchin, D. (1994) *Post-traumatic Stress Disorder: A Practical Guide to Recovery.* London: HarperCollins.

Kinchin, D. (2004) *Post Traumatic Stress Disorder: The Invisible Injury.* Oxon: Success Unlimited.

Kirschenbaum, H. and Henderson, V. (eds) (1996) *The Carl Rogers Reader.* London: Constable.

Mitchell, J. and Everly, G.S. (2001) *Critical Incident Stress Debriefing.* Ellicott City: Chevron.

Parkinson, F. (1997) *Critical Incident Debriefing: Understanding and Dealing with Trauma.* London: Souvenir Press.

Raphael, B. and Wilson, J. (2000) *Psychological Debriefing: Theory, Practice and Evidence.* Cambridge: Cambridge University Press.

Saari, S. (2005) *A Bolt from the Blue: Coping with Disasters and Acute Traumas.* London: Jessica Kingsley Publishers.

Yule, W. and Gold, A. (1997) 'The *Herald of Free Enterprise* Disaster.' In D. Blackman, M. Newman, J. Harris-Hendricks and G. Mezey (eds) *Psychological Trauma: A Developmental Approach.* London: Gaskell.

CHAPTER FOUR

Defusing

Although this text is primarily concerned with psychological debriefing, it is necessary to spend a little time discussing and explaining defusing if only to prevent the two from becoming mixed up.

The term may appear to be a little unusual but 'defusing' is something that many of us practise on a regular basis. When children fall over and hurt themselves, they will often come running to the nearest known adult for a cuddle. The injured limb may be inspected and reassuring words will be uttered. In the good old days, Nanny used to 'kiss it better', and such action would usually stop the tears and be rewarded with a smile and runny nose. In essence, this cuddle and sympathy is a very normal form of defusing. It is practised worldwide in all cultures and we have probably all done it.

Structured defusing

In the adult world, it isn't appropriate to wander around kissing people better. Adults need some sort of structure for the 'tea and sympathy' support, which is offered to those who have suffered a shock or traumatic event.

When compared with a similar model for debriefing (see Figure 3.5 on p.74), it can be seen from Figure 4.1 that the course of a defusing is less likely to become embroiled in the emotional side of the event. It will stick much more to the facts and the immediate consequences of an incident or traumatic event.

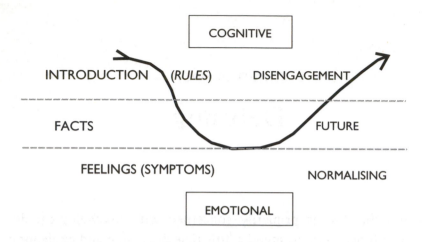

Figure 4.1: The defusing process (adapted from Mitchell and Everly 2001)

The term 'defusing' was introduced by Mitchell and Everly in 1983. They said that they chose the word because it suggested that a dangerous or difficult situation was being rendered harmless. Today this term is given to a small-group process that usually occurs within a few hours of the incident (on the same day at least). It is a much shortened form of psychological debriefing and offers people the opportunity to talk briefly about their experiences before they have time to rethink the incident and reinterpret its meaning. The process of defusing is far less structured than debriefing and consequently it is much easier to organise and facilitate.

Defusing usually takes between 20 minutes and one hour.

Tehrani (2004) describes defusing in a work environment as having eight goals:

1. The rapid reduction of intense reactions to the traumatic event.

2. The normalising of the experience, enabling people to return to normal life as quickly as possible.

3. The re-establishment of the social network of the working group so that employees do not isolate themselves from each other.

4. The sharing of information about the incident between all the people involved.

5. The restoration of cognitive processes disrupted by the incident.

6. The provision of practical information for dealing with stress, and traumatic stress reactions.

7. An affirmation of the value of every member of staff, both to one another, and to the organisation.

8. The development of an expectancy of recovery. (Adapted from the Post Office model, Noreen Tehrani [2004], although Noreen herself claims to hate it being given that title as it has been used with plenty of other organisations too. Readers will be aware that organisations such as post offices and banks attract their own peculiar traumas when the organisation is robbed.)

Each defusing will be different. Sometimes people will have a great deal to say, sometimes there will be very little said. However, as the group relaxes, they tend to give more details of their experience. The group leader should be both confident and competent to take the defusing process through the three basic stages of Introduction, Exploration and Information. The three stages are explained much more fully in the debriefing section of this module, but a short guide is provided here:

Introduction

This first section motivates people and outlines the guidelines which make the process run safely and smoothly. For example, the people present are assured that the defusing team (there are usually two defusers present at any one defusing) will not take notes or make reports of the discussion to anyone. What is discussed during a defusing is held in the strictest of confidence.

Exploration

Exploration is the second phase of a structured defusing. The incident is described by the participants in very broad terms and each person listens to the others in turn as they describe things from their own perspective. It is usually possible to get some sort of chronology of events in this phase of the defusing.

Information

This third and final phase of defusing is critical. The defusing team explains what an acute stress reaction might mean to people, exploring some of the possible symptoms. This is forewarning people of what might happen if they go on to suffer with a reaction which may develop into Post-Traumatic Stress Disorder (PTSD). There is a strong emphasis here on what is normal. It is very normal to react to a traumatic event.

Table 4.1 shows the typical time allocation for a defusing.

Table 4.1 The typical time allocation for a defusing

Stage	Percentage	Typical time
Introduction	20	10 minutes
Exploration	50	25 minutes
Information	30	15 minutes

Effects of defusing

There are two desirable effects of a defusing which are typical in almost all cases. The effects depend upon the correct application of the defusing within an appropriate time-frame (the same day as the distressing event). A carefully applied and well-managed defusing will usually either eliminate the need to do a debriefing or enhance a debriefing if it is still necessary.

Mitchell warns, however, that the elimination of a need to provide a psychological debriefing is a by-product of a defusing, not a goal. In other words, it may happen naturally but one is not working to achieve that effect.

Simple or formal defusing

Parkinson (1997) advocates the idea of two different types of defusing, which can be used according to need. Clearly, the more formal defusing might be applied to a more significant traumatic event, and the simple version delivered following moderately traumatic events.

Table 4.2 suggests a structure for the simpler version.

Table 4.2 Simple defusing

Venue	Defuser provides a safe and confidential environment. Makes sure that people are comfortable, and refreshments available.
Introduction	Defuser suggests that it will help to talk. Is sympathetic. Allows people time to relax.
Facts	Where were you before, during and after the incident? What happened? What did you do?
Feelings	How did you react? How did you feel at the time? How did you feel later, when it was over? How are you now?
Future	Defuser reassures participants about the normality of their reactions. What do you feel you need – if anything? Are you ready to go back to work/on duty?

Assess whether a full debriefing is required at a later date.

Source: Parkinson 1997

Formal defusing is, according to Parkinson (1997), more structured than the simple version. The defuser should:

1. ask about participants' reactions

2. comment positively about their performance

3. not allow undue criticism

4. attempt to reduce excessive black humour

5. be aware of defence mechanisms

6. mention that a psychological debriefing may follow.

All this is in addition to the steps suggested for a simple defusing. The formal defusing may last between 30 minutes and an hour whereas the simple defusing is probably only going to take 20–25 minutes.

Defusing is usually seen as the forerunner to a psychological debriefing and is all part of the trauma package that organisations should have in place to deal with traumatic events. Neither a defusing nor a debriefing should be seen as a stand-alone option and a quick fix for those who have suffered a traumatic experience. It is because some organisations have tried to use these processes in isolation that the procedures have, in some quarters, been given a bad press.

Bibliography

Mitchell, J. and Everly, G.S. (2001) *Critical Incident Stress Debriefing.* Ellicott City: Chevron.

Parkinson, F. (1997) *Critical Incident Debriefing: Understanding and Dealing with Trauma.* London: Souvenir Press.

Saari, S. (2005) *A Bolt from the Blue: Coping with Disasters and Acute Traumas.* London: Jessica Kingsley Publishers.

Tehrani, N. (2004) *Workplace Trauma: Concepts, Assessment and Interventions.* New York: Brunner-Routledge.

CHAPTER FIVE

Recovery from Post-Traumatic Stress Disorder

It is important that anyone who defuses or debriefs a group has a good working knowledge of Post-Traumatic Stress Disorder (PTSD) and recovery from the disorder. It is important to focus on the positive state of recovery. There is a twenty-first century trend to try and illustrate behaviours by producing models for that behaviour. There are also models to show chemical reactions and climatological patterns. Few people, however, have tried to show recovery from PTSD in the form of a model. Research for this module has managed to find only three clear models which show recovery from PTSD. Each has its strengths and weaknesses and it is left for you to decide which is the most appropriate.

Perhaps the most common question asked by PTSD survivors after 'Am I going mad?' is 'When will I get better?' It is a perfectly natural question. If a person suffers appendicitis or a broken leg, there is a typical recovery period and there are definite stages before good health is regained. Stitches are removed or the plaster cast is taken off. With PTSD, there are no such readily identifiable stages of recovery and each individual's progress will be different.

Models of recovery

In Williams' (1993) model (see Figure 5.1), the first phase of PTSD is described as the initial trauma (stressor) and the initial immobilisation and denial that are the main characteristics of this phase. This phase covers the initial shock of the trauma.

The second phase, or impact phase, is characterised by chronic stress reactions. Flashbacks and all the associated symptoms are usually experienced during this phase.

The third stage is the recovery or resolution phase. This involves the survivor 'testing' situations that were previously avoided because of their association with the original stressor. Finally, there is an acceptance of the trauma and an integration of the traumatic memory as part of a life memory.

Unfortunately, Williams' model falls far short of characterising the general stages of recovery by the PTSD survivor. The timescale of recovery is seldom regular – yet Williams' model suggests it can be. Williams' placing of symptoms such as anger and depression within the impact phase also gives an erroneous impression that anger is far more significant than depression. It suggests a set pattern of recovery, yet fails to provide an accurate timescale for these phases. The model would appear to ask as many questions as it answers.

Horowitz (1979) also produced a model showing the phases of response following a trauma (see Figure 5.2). The model extends from the initial outcry of the traumatic incident, through a state of denial, intrusive memories and working through what happened, until completion is reached, although Horowitz does allow a period of oscillation between some states.

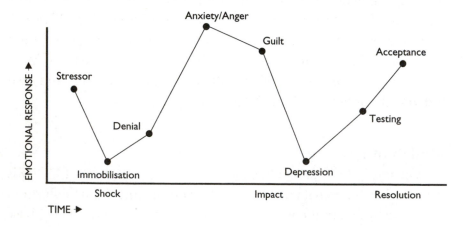

Figure 5.1: Model of PTSD recovery (adapted from Williams 1993)

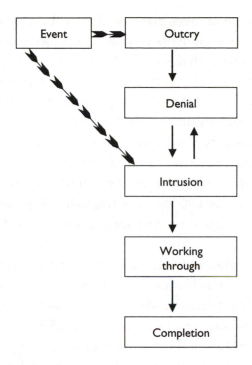

Figure 5.2: Phases of response following a trauma (adapted from Horowitz 1979)

Once again, this model is far too simple, and does not tell the full story. Furthermore, it also assumes that eventually the impact of the trauma will disappear. More recent work suggests this is not the case (Kinchin 1998). Like a physical wound, which leaves some scar tissue as a reminder of the injury, victims of trauma incorporate the event into their life experience with psychological scarring. So, even with full recovery, they are never likely to return to how they were before the event.

The snakes and ladders model of recovery (see Figure 5.3)

In many ways, PTSD sufferers find themselves playing a game of emotional snakes and ladders. The game board represents the road to recovery, divided into 100 squares. A series of ladders helps the person on the way towards recovery but between these ladders are the snakes, which may take the victim backwards towards the start of the game, and to re-experience previous anguish and turmoil.

The traumatic event takes place on Square 1. From this position, recovery begins. Some survivors may shake the dice scoring five, four, three and then one to reach Square 100, thus achieving recovery in just four shakes of the dice. In less than four weeks, these people have recovered from the trauma and they do *not* go on to develop PTSD. Other survivors have to journey around the board going up the ladders and down the snakes as they slowly progress to the end of the game.

Tragically, some people may never finish the game.

Furthermore, they may never roll the correct number on the dice to finish exactly on Square 100, or, more tragically, they may give up and walk away from the game board taking unrelinquished trauma with them.

The game of snakes and ladders is very complex. Study the game board in detail. It is possible for a player to be on Square 97, only to shake a one, two, five, five, five and one. These throws take a player back to Square 4! Thankfully, on a true snakes and ladders board, no single snake can take a person all the way back to the start square.

So a person can finish the game in four moves or they can be taken back 94 squares in just six moves. Describing PTSD in such a way may

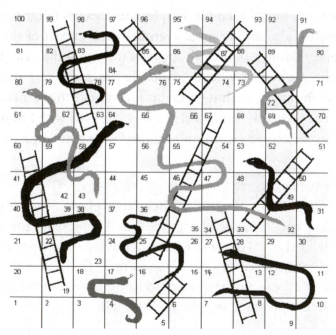

Figure 5.3: Snakes and ladders model of recovery (Kinchin 1994, 1998, 2004)

give a greater insight into the complicated road to recovery from PTSD. This analogy is probably more realistic than the very simple idea that recovery is a case of two steps forward and then one step back. Recovery is not smooth; neither is it predictable, and it will incorporate a wealth of stages which extend far beyond the models described by Williams and Horowitz.

EXAMPLES OF SNAKES AND LADDERS WHICH MIGHT AFFECT A PERSON'S RECOVERY

Ladders

- Good medication, such as antidepressants, can be seen as an essential aid to recovery for many survivors. The withdrawal of medication has to be slow and sympathetic or this 'ladder' can quickly become a 'snake'.
- Therapy, which includes counselling and any other form of support in which the client has confidence, is helpful (Kinchin 1997).
- Relaxation techniques can be taught and practised.
- Realisation that there is a 'trauma bond' (a feeling of empathy which exists between those who have suffered traumatic events). It is a realisation that 'you are not alone' and 'you are not going mad'.
- Individual or group support is an essential part of recovery.
- Meeting a counsellor or other therapist who shows real empathic appreciation of the situation.

Snakes

- Panic attacks can become a major 'snake' in the path of recovery. Because the fear of panic is so great, many survivors develop avoidance strategies in an attempt to stay away from anything that might cause a panic attack.
- Depression can manifest itself any time. A deep trough of depression can cause a survivor to walk away from the game board altogether.

- Triggers – something which instantly reminds the person of the trauma. This may be a sound, a smell or a particular situation.

- Alcohol and non-prescribed drugs can act as an initial 'crutch', but dependency on these products can seriously hinder any real progress towards recovery.

- Adverse publicity can heighten the state of a survivor's feelings of guilt.

- Anniversaries are often obstacles, but a successfully handled anniversary can also be turned into a very positive milestone towards recovery.

- Non-acceptance of PTSD by professionals and lay people can be a serious problem for survivors who feel the severity of the traumatic response is being disregarded or belittled.

These examples illustrate some of the events and issues which may affect people on the road to recovery. Many PTSD sufferers tend to set themselves goals or targets. Often these targets will be linked to the calendar:

- 'I will return to work by 1st June.'

- 'I want to have stopped sleeping with the main light on by Christmas.'

- 'I intend to go out shopping on my own during the holiday weekend.'

Formulating goals and targets is a very good strategy provided the targets are within reach. If the target is too difficult, then the sufferer is in danger of setting unrealistic goals that serve no useful purpose. Rather, sufferers should be encouraged to set themselves sensible, attainable, targets. Dates for accomplishing tasks should be within a reasonable timescale. If the target is reached before the date, a treat may act as a positive reward. For children in particular, it is vital they are enabled to achieve small steps towards recovery.

Inevitably, some targets will not be achieved. Unpredictable events may hinder progress – that's life! Therefore, unexpected events should be allowed for in the preparation of targets, and breathing spaces need to be included between achieving a goal and embarking on the next hurdle. Targets are wonderful when they are achieved, but terrible if the sufferer is defeated by them.

The snakes and ladders board can act as a helpful reminder to the client of their journey towards recovery. If they fail to reach a target, that failure does not drag them all the way back to Square 1. Even in failing, they have learned something about how best to set the next target.

FULL RECOVERY

It is not necessary to reach Square 100 on the snakes and ladders board to have recovered from PTSD. Indeed, it is suggested that in some cases reaching Square 100 is not possible. Being involved in a seriously traumatic event affects the rest of a survivor's life. This may require a person to rethink life goals or life values.

Perhaps it would be useful to consider full recovery as anything beyond Square 91 on the game board. If we return to the example of a broken leg cited earlier, there is always the thought in the back of a person's mind that the leg could break again. Likewise with PTSD, some of the symptoms could be awakened if triggers occur. Therefore, reaching the top nine squares on the snakes and ladders board, while being aware of the remaining two snakes, may be perceived as recovery.

Traumatic anniversaries

We live in a society where anniversaries and special dates are important. Not only are they important but they are big business. We celebrate birthdays and wedding anniversaries every year. These are frequently very public anniversaries. We may celebrate our first date, our first kiss or the first time we made love, but these celebrations are often strictly limited to those who are involved. They are private.

As a society, we very publicly remember the important dates in past conflicts. Various military operations and battles have a special memory for some, but on 11 November every year we remember those who lost their lives fighting for their beliefs. This is an example of a very public celebration or act of remembrance, and the memory is often a traumatic one.

The benchmark for traumatic memories has traditionally been the assassination of President Kennedy on 22 November 1963. 'Where were you when you heard the news that Kennedy had been shot?' is the well-rehearsed and much repeated question. The assumption is that it was such a traumatic occurrence that everyone remembers it very clearly. In more recent times, the same could be said for the terrorist attack on the twin towers in New York – 9/11. We can link to this the tragic road accident which killed Princess Diana on 31 August 1997. These events really allowed people to wear their hearts on their sleeves. Public expressions of emotion became acceptable, overnight.

On a very private level, there are many people who suffer in silence as they remember their own traumatic anniversary. As traumatic anniversaries exist for so many people, it is something of a surprise that their debilitating effects are not more widely accepted and understood.

For those who have suffered a serious and potentially life-threatening trauma, that memory will remain with them throughout their lives. Those who develop PTSD will usually receive support in the form of counselling or psychotherapy of some kind. That support doesn't last forever, although anniversaries of that traumatic event will come around every single year of their lives.

Every day of every week of the year, someone somewhere is reliving the memory of their specific trauma. This may be a large-scale disaster, which whole populations will recall, or it may be a very small-scale incident, which involved just one or two people but was equally traumatic for those who lived it at the time.

There are no rules about anniversaries. Without doubt, the most painful traumatic anniversary is the first one. That is usually a major milestone and for many it is a considerable hurdle to overcome. Once survived, that first milestone can be looked back on as a hurdle successfully negotiated. But first it has to be overcome.

Time is reported as being a great healer. For many people that is true and subsequent anniversaries may have less of an impact on their lives. But that should not be expected as the norm because when dealing with traumatic memories there really is no norm – everyone is different. Just because the eighth anniversary passed without a hitch doesn't necessarily mean that the ninth will be a pushover. It doesn't always work that way.

So the next time a work colleague takes a day's sick leave with back pains or a migraine, don't simply dismiss it. Stop and think. Are they taking a 'sickie'? Are they suffering with back pain or a migraine? Or are they enduring yet another anniversary of the event they experienced, the traumatic memory of which they have still not yet managed to deal with?

When it comes to anniversaries, nobody should be too quick to judge!

Difficulties

Occasionally, PTSD victims have encountered the following difficulties:

- Making unreasonable generalisations (e.g. 'All men are sexual abusers'; 'Every teacher is a bully').

- Mentally filtering aspects of their trauma. Seizing on a particularly gloomy aspect of an event and dwelling on it (e.g. 'He could have been killed doing that').

- Believing 'all or nothing'. Everything is seen in the most extreme terms (e.g. 'I am either in control or I am not').

- Labelling themselves. Individuals focus on their emotional state and draw conclusions about themselves (e.g. 'Since it happened, I am frightened of my own shadow, I guess I am just a wimp').

- A discounting attitude. Disregarding any positive outcomes (e.g. 'I did my best, so what?').

- Magnification and minimisation of self-worth. Shortcomings are emphasised and strengths are made light of (e.g. 'Since the trauma I am so irritable with my parents, and just about manage to keep going to school').

- Making 'should' statements. Inappropriate use of moral imperatives – should; must; have; ought (e.g. 'It's ridiculous that since the attack I have to take my sister shopping with me. I *should* be able to do this by myself').

- Jumping to conclusions (e.g. 'Everyone thinks I should be over this by now').

- Over-personalisation of the situation. Assuming that because something went wrong it must be the survivor's fault (e.g. 'I must have made a mistake somewhere for him to have died').

Advice for those in early recovery (after Quinton [1994] and others)

These comments are based on personal experiences and, although there is no research evidence to support them all, there is sufficient un-researched information to justify their inclusion here. There is a marked difference between the comments about survivors who have just set out on the road to recovery, and the comments describing those who have almost completed the journey and are in advanced stages of recovery.

Aileen Quinton, whose mother died in the Enniskillen bombing, suggests that a person suffering from PTSD should:

- claim the right to experience and to express their own feelings

- allow themselves to cry, because it can be very therapeutic

- take every opportunity to talk if this is helpful

- remember that it is the situation that is abnormal, not the trauma that is felt

- make contact with others in a similar situation in order to feel relieved at how similar other victims' feelings may be (the trauma bond)

- be encouraged to progress in an individual way and at their own pace, taking 'breathing spaces' after achieving goals or accepting temporary regression of progress if necessary

- be prevented from 'pushing themselves' too quickly in an attempt to please others

- be empowered to make their own decisions.

Summary

When supporting children or adults, it is believed that the snakes and ladders model is an approach that can be applied to all individuals because:

- it allows for the oscillations in recovery described by Horowitz (1979)

- it is easy to comprehend, because almost everyone has some knowledge of the snakes and ladders game

- the process of recovery is easily explained

- although the snakes and ladders model appears to be very simple, the model also demonstrates the complexity of PTSD, allowing for extremes of the disorder.

Bibliography

Horowitz, M.J. (1979) 'Psychological Response to Serious Life Events.' In V. Hamilton and D. Warburton (eds) *Human Stress and Cognition: An Information Processing Approach.* New York: Wiley.

Kinchin, D. (1994) *Post Traumatic Stress Disorder: A Practical Guide to Recovery.* London: HarperCollins.

Kinchin, D. (1997) 'Post Traumatic Stress Disorder: Aromatherapy and physiotherapy can be a prelude to effective counselling.' *Alternative Therapies in Clinical Practice 4, 2, 55–56.*

Kinchin, D. (1998, 2004) *Post Traumatic Stress Disorder: The Invisible Injury.* Oxon: Success Unlimited.

Quinton, A. (1994) Unpublished lecture notes.

Scott, M.J. and Palmer, S. (2000) *Trauma and Post-traumatic Stress Disorder.* London: Cassell.

Williams, T. (1993) 'Trauma in the Workplace.' In J.P. Wilson and B. Raphael (eds) *International Handbook of Traumatic Stress.* New York: Plenum Press.

CHAPTER SIX

Training for Debriefers

Training for debriefers

The training of debriefers has suffered because there is no standard, and currently there is no such thing as an accredited debriefer. Looking at the work of the British Psychological Society and their report on psychological debriefing (Tehrani 2002), it is clear that there are vast differences in the training of debriefers both nationally and internationally.

Setting a standard for debriefing training and for the clinical supervision of debriefers may be some way off. I am concerned that those who attempt to set the standards have their own agendas for doing so (perhaps I have my own agenda too), but something along the lines suggested here may be appropriate:

	Initial Training	Four-day course
Year 1	Annual update	One-day refresher
Year 2	Biannual refresher	Two-day course
	Years 1 and 2 repeated	

Supervision of individual debriefers needs to take place regularly – after every three debriefing sessions or annually if fewer sessions have been facilitated during that time. The supervision could form part of the annual one-day update. Currently, it would appear that very few debriefers receive the level of clinical supervision they should expect and require.

Code of ethics for debriefing

At the time of writing, no such code exists. This is a gap which needs to be filled. Currently, the work of debriefers relies upon the integrity of those individuals and organisations that provide the service.

The following training course has been tried and tested, and proven to be a very good way of training peer debriefers who have a keen interest in supporting their co-workers. They come to the course with no previous experience of active listening or counselling, but they have a willingness to learn. The course is devised to teach the skills that will be required to debrief a group. These skills are complemented with a knowledge of Post-Traumatic Stress Disorder (PTSD) and a familiarisation with the different debriefing models which abound today. One model is taught in depth, but students are encouraged to explore other models in their own time (if they so wish).

There is a heavy emphasis on practical skills and almost half the four-day course is spent learning and practising debriefing skills on each other. The students are also tested and encouraged to exorcise any demons that they have in their past. There is plenty of time to talk openly and confidentially about issues from their past that have caused alarm and distress. It is a very exhausting course and it is always recommended that the course starts on a Tuesday, so that when it finishes on Friday the students will have a weekend break before they return to work.

Training course in detail (maximum 18 students)

Day one

An initial introduction and welcome to the course is usually made by someone well respected within the organisation. The tutor(s) is introduced to the course and their qualifications for leading the course are shared. This demonstrates the openness with which the course is run throughout the four days.

The first main teaching session is about PTSD. This session will include information about the definition and causes of PTSD, the symptoms of the disorder and an explanation of recovery using the snakes and ladders model to demonstrate this. This may be illustrated with a

DVD of a particular traumatic event appropriate to the work of the students on the course.

The rest of the day is spent learning and then practising active listening skills. The students will be taught how best to reflect, prompt, summarise and focus their participants (Stage One listening skills). They will also receive some teaching about the use of empathy, immediacy and challenging (Stage Two listening skills). Finally (Stage Three listening skills), the course explores goals, prioritising and referrals. It may be appropriate to refer to a simple counselling skills text to illustrate these very useful skills. The students often find these are skills which they already have, and use, but have not explored or specifically named.

During the course of the teaching of these skills, the group will often be split into trios to practise – one student being the practitioner, one the client and the third the observer. Each has a definite task and an important role to play in the teaching of these very practical skills. Skills sessions last about 45 minutes with each student in turn being allowed to play each of the three roles. The items brought to the trio by the client might be 'something I have lost recently' or 'something or someone who recently annoyed me'.

The day concludes with a 'washing-up' session to clarify any issues that may have arisen. Students are reminded again about the confidentiality of any material shared in the trio practical sessions.

Day two

The day starts in much the same way as the previous day ended, with a chance for any questions on what has been learned so far. This is followed by a couple of simple practical exercises to get students used to challenging their clients in the appropriate way. This usually acts as a good icebreaker to the second day. Students should be beginning to know each other and trust each other by this time.

Some teaching on Complex PTSD, Dual Attention Theory and the way PTSD can affect people is then delivered. This may be complemented with DVD material. A general discussion is then encouraged where the students consider the advantages and disadvantages of peer debriefing versus debriefing by a professional outsider to the organisation.

The second half of the second day sees the first teaching on the theory of psychological debriefing itself. It is advisable to introduce students (at a very basic level) to three or four different debriefing models, and illustrate some of the basic similarities and differences.

The tutor then leads a practical session showing the students how an introduction to a debriefing might go.

Other DVD material might be introduced before the final session of the day goes back to working in trios and discussing 'Someone dear to me has died'.

There is a washing-up session at the very end of the day.

Day three

This launches straight into the rest of the debriefing theory explaining the various stages of a debriefing session in considerable detail and illustrating each stage with as many practical examples as possible. If the tutor is a good storyteller, this makes the session an easier one. It is nonetheless intensive.

This session is followed by a practical one exploring the endings of a debriefing session and what the content of the teaching element of a debriefing might be. By the end of this, the students should be familiar with the introductions and the conclusions of a debrief, but they will not yet have explored for themselves the middle stage of a debriefing.

A quiz might be introduced at this stage. As well as testing what has been learned, this is a time for students to gather their own thoughts and focus on what they have learned. Experience has taught that this is the stage that any 'drop-outs' from the course are likely to occur. It is now that they fully realise what debriefing will demand of them.

Brief discussions take place about 'supervision' of debriefers and exactly what supervision means in this context. Codes of ethics are also discussed; perhaps the tutor may use the codes of ethics used by the British Association of Counsellors and Psychotherapists (BACP) or the Association of Christian Counsellors (ACC).

Finally, a short session about defusing will be the final one of the day.

It may be that there is time now to prepare for the practical sessions of the last day – if not, then these will take place first thing on the final morning.

Day four

This day is devoted to practical debriefing. With 18 delegates, they can be divided into three groups. At any one time in each group, there will be two co-debriefers and four people who will participate as clients to be debriefed. This means that, by the end of three 75-minute sessions, everyone will have been a client twice and a debriefer once. Everyone will have some shared experience of three debriefing sessions.

The scenario for the debriefing requires careful planning by the tutor. There needs to be sufficient information (either in DVD or note format) for the students to be able to play-act a little and put themselves in the position of a client attending a debriefing. If three slightly different scenarios can be given, then that adds interest to the day.

The tutor ideally needs two assistants for this day, so that each of the three practical debriefings can be monitored and observed, and some useful advice and comment can be made in the end session of each debrief. The feedback at the end of each debriefing is usually significant and well received by both the debriefers and the clients.

It is very tiring to work through three debriefing sessions in one day – tiring for everyone involved. However, the final session of the day – of the course – needs to be full of practical local information about how people might be contacted and asked to run a debriefing for a group. These local details may be brought to the training session by a welfare officer or human resources manager who will be tasked with setting up the debriefing sessions and perhaps deciding which events warrant holding a debriefing.

At the very end of the training course, it is important to have a little bit of fun, and so awards for the 'super swot' who gained the most points in the quiz, and for the 'drama queen' who has consistently been the best role-player during the day, can now be awarded to let off steam. The students will be very tired by this stage.

This course has run over four eight-hour days. It is an exhausting course, but it has proved to work effectively time and time again. The drop-out rate for the course averages at slightly less than one student per course. In every instance, this dropping out has been due to something in the course reminding the student of an event in their lives – there was 'unfinished business', which had not been dealt with properly at the time and would probably have reared its ugly head at some time in the future. Students who do drop out of this course need the tender love and care of their supervisor or welfare officer. They should not be left to their own devices unless they specifically say that is what they want.

As a tutor, I have delivered this course on a number of occasions to a variety of different groups. The course can be modified (i.e. reduced in time) if it is being run for a group who already have considerable counselling skills.

Refresher courses

Refresher courses are usually delivered to remind students of skills previously taught. That, though, is not enough. Debriefing refresher courses should perhaps include some teaching on transference and counter-transference, which debriefers will have come across in their work. Refresher courses can in effect become a chance to debrief the debriefers, to share issues (remembering confidentiality of clients) and to discuss any difficult situations that have presented themselves.

Experience has shown that about 90 per cent of all live debriefings run without a hitch. The remaining 10 per cent may have an uneasy feel about them for a while, and that is usually because of a lack of information given to the debriefer or a pre-existing issue among the group of clients. No debriefing can be foolproof but, if working to achieve 'best practice', then each slight mishap should be investigated and explored in an attempt to make sure that the same mistake is not repeated. Learning about debriefing is an organic experience that grows at a fascinating rate.

Attending a refresher course may offer a debriefer an opportunity for some supervision work on a one-to-one basis with the tutor. Alternatively, supervision can be offered in small groups. This latter suggestion holds considerable merit and provides debriefers with an opportunity to fine-tune their debriefing style by listening to what works and doesn't work for their fellow debriefers. If debriefers are used to working in pairs or threes, then there should be no reason why supervision should not be undertaken in similar small groups.

In 2002, the British Psychological Society produced a working party report (Tehrani 2002) that explored many different aspects of psychological debriefing. There is a two-page appendix to the report, which attempts to tabulate the state of psychological debriefing around the world. The table includes such details as the length of time an organisation has been providing debriefing, which model they might use and what protocols or procedures are in place. The final entries to this table are under the headings 'length of training' and 'supervision', and these two columns reveal the terrible truth that there isn't actually much done by way of training people to become debriefers, and those who are trained are offered very little in the form of supervision sessions. It is a hope that during the intervening years things have changed, that organisations have vastly improved the training offered to debriefers (whether professional debriefers or peer debriefers) and that the availability and quality of the supervision have vastly improved too.

Bibliography

Tehrani, N. (ed.) (2002) *Psychological Debriefing: Professional Proactive Board Working Party Report.* Leicester: The British Psychological Society.

Psychological Debriefing – An Effective Method?

(Reproduced here with the kind permission of Atle Dyregrov PhD)

The critique of Psychological Debriefing and its setting

Psychological Debriefing (PD), also termed Critical Incident Debriefing (CID), or Emotional Decompression (ED), or Critical Incident Stress Debriefing (CISD), was originally described by Mitchell in 1983 as 'either an individual or group meeting between the rescue worker and the caring individual (facilitator) who is able to help the person talk about his feelings and reactions to the critical incident'.

Some of the conceptual confusions originated in Mitchell using the term debrief for individual contacts although he later referred to CISD as 'a group meeting for discussion about a distressing critical incident' (Mitchell and Everly 1998). Dyregrov (1989a) presented the following definition: 'A psychological debriefing is a group meeting arranged for the purpose of integrating profound personal experiences both on the cognitive, emotional and group level, and thus preventing the development of adverse reaction.'

A detailed review of facts, thoughts, impressions and reactions can obviously be used in conversations with individuals as part of normal crisis intervention, while psychological debriefing as a method was designed for groups. For group meetings to achieve their aims they should be instigated within a brief time after the traumatic event, those who lead the group must be trained and experienced in leading the debrief process, the group must have experienced a common stressor, time must allow a thorough review of the different 'phases', and the meetings used to screen those who need extra help. The many factors influencing the debrief meeting and its ability to achieve its purpose is described in Dyregrov (1997). From Mitchell's (1983) first description of the method until today's practice there have been significant changes, and presently the method usually is used as one part of a more integrated system of interventions referred to as Critical Incident Stress Management or CISM (Mitchell and Everly 1998).

In recent years several critical reports have been published regarding the use of PD, CID, or CISD. A heated debate has been going on both in Australia, the United States and in Great Britain, even leading to a suggested discontinuation of the use of CISD protocols (see Avery and Orner 1998). Since the debate continues in some unenlightened circles and has led to premature suggestions for discontinuation of the use of PD it is necessary to look more closely at some of these studies.

The above mentioned debate grew rapidly after Beverly Raphael, Leonore Meldrum and Alexander C. McFarlane wrote a rather 'unfortunate' letter to the editor of the *British Medical Journal* back in 1995, asking for more randomised controlled studies of the method. Furthermore, they stated that several studies reported a negative effect of the method. In addition they wrote that the method actually could aggravate the traumatic process, and that it has an ideological and symbolic more than a helping value. Several studies reviewed later in this article were also taken as 'proof' that PD has no effect. Raphael, Meldrum and McFarlane are respected experts in the traumatology field, and their reservations against debriefing naturally left many professionals in doubt about the necessity and effectiveness of debriefings. In this article it is proposed that their critique was based on studies that did not warrant the negative presentation they gave of debriefing.

Studies reporting no effect of debriefing

In the following an evaluation will be presented of the studies that purport that PD or CISD does not have the desired effect. Following this a description of studies supporting PD is given.

Deahl *et al.* (1994) investigated the proneness for disease in soldiers from the first Gulf War, finding that debriefing did not reduce later psychiatric morbidity. They do not make clear what the debriefing consisted of since the intervention is only briefly mentioned in the article. They furthermore inform the reader that they have used Dyregrov's model (1989b). This is rather strange since neither has this author developed such a model, nor have this group received training from me. In addition the timing of the debriefing is highly variable. The most serious methodological objection is, however, the self-selection that has taken place to the debriefing group. This means that the participants in the debriefing group personally wanted to take part in the debriefing, most likely as a result of a greater need to talk about the event than the individuals who automatically became part of a control group. This of course becomes a serious source of error that may explain the possible differences between the groups. The authors themselves are aware of these methodological limitations, and conclude, despite their negative results, that: '...despite our findings we remain committed to the principle of debriefing...'. They emphasise the importance of a rapid and locally held debriefing, and that the soldiers were suspicious towards 'outsiders', including mental health personnel.

In Australia, Justin Kenardy and colleagues (1996) have conducted research on rescue personnel after an earthquake. They found no effect of the debriefing during the two years following the disaster (measured with GHQ-12 and IES on four different occasions). The groups were established through self-selection with the sources of error this entails and that already are commented upon. The participants taking part in the debriefing group were significantly different from the control group regarding level of education, their self-report on being helpful in non-threatening situations, by having higher professional prestige, and by being more females (females usually report more distress on most measures, cf. Breslau *et al.* 1997). The authors had no control over the debriefing procedures, thus it is not known what they consisted of. Furthermore, background and training of the debriefing leaders is not documented, and the same goes for the timing of the debriefing. The authors report that 80 per cent of the participants felt that the debriefing was of help.

In Great Britain, Lee, Slade and Lygo (1996) have offered what they call 'Psychological Debriefing' to women having had a miscarriage. In this study the women were randomised to two different groups and they were offered a one-hour consultation in their own home two weeks following the miscarriage. It is obvious that they had emphasised a schematic procedure in the various phases of the debriefing. One week and four months after this consultation the women were screened for anxiety, depression, intrusive memories and avoidance reactions. This screening showed no differences between the groups. This study is peculiar in several ways. First of all, it is not a study of debriefing. It does not describe how a group of subjects, being gathered for intervention following a disaster they all have been involved in, is coping. It could have been a description of a crisis intervention if the help had arrived earlier. However, the most serious aspect of this study is that the women only were offered a one-hour consultation following their miscarriage. The author of this article has for many years worked with families who had lost a child. The follow-up necessary in such situations demands a much more intensive approach (Dyregrov 1989a, 1990). It is indeed very doubtful whether the PD format is adequate in a one-hour follow-up in these situations. A short conversation around a very emotionally demanding situation may open up emotional channels without adequate time to talk through the event.

Hobbs *et al.* (1996) randomised a group of victims after traffic accidents to an intervention group and a control group. The intervention consisted of what the authors called psychological debriefing which lasted for one hour, and it was usually carried out between 24 and 48 hours following the accident. While the groups were not different regarding symptoms preceding the intervention, the intervention group had experienced more serious physical injuries following the accident and they stayed longer in hospital than the controls. Four months following the intervention the researchers found no significant decline in different symptoms in any of the two groups.

In two sub-scales of the 'Brief Symptom Inventory' the intervention group had higher scores (more problems). The intervention is carried out individually and not in a group, and the session lasts for one hour only, without any follow-up. This is more a study of crisis intervention of dubious quality more than it is a study of debriefing. Clinically it is also questionable whether the use of an intervention following the 'debriefing model' is correct at this point in time following the event. This author's clinical experience has been that the physical healing must take place before the psychological healing processes can continue. That they in this study try to pressure the wounded person into cognitive and emotional processing of the accident is a questionable clinical procedure in my opinion. It seems quite clear that this and the previously mentioned studies look at the effect of one hour of individual consultation, more than study the effect of PD.

Bisson *et al.* (1997) randomised patients wounded in a fire to what they called a debrief-group and a control group. The intervention was given to each single patient or couples, and it lasted on average 44 minutes (30–120 minutes), and was carried out by a nurse or a research psychiatrist who were tutored by the first author (psychiatrist). The results showed that 16 (26%) of the PD group was found to have PTSD following 13 months, while in the control group 9 per cent were diagnosed with PTSD. Even before the intervention, the PD group was described as having experienced twice as many important past traumas, and in addition the PD group had experienced more serious fire traumas than the control group. Both these aspects can explain why the PD group's PTSD diagnoses were higher in number than for the control group. Turnbull, Busuttil and Pittman (1997) have raised several other methodological objections against this study. Bisson and co-workers also reported that the earlier the intervention was carried out following the accident, the worse they were doing later on. This pertains to the criticism raised against Hobbs and colleagues – it is clinically unsound to intervene following PD principles while physical healing is taking place. In a letter to the *British Journal of Psychiatry* following this study, a doctor who himself had been wounded in a fire stated that the timing of PD was incorrect (Kraus 1997).

A question should also be raised regarding the type of quick intervention that took place in the study by Bisson *et al.* Paramount when practising PD is to spend the amount of time required. In this study 44 minutes on average was spent with the patients. Within this short amount of time the author of this article would not even have finished listening to the participants telling the facts and thoughts regarding the event. If anything is measured in Bisson *et al.*'s study, it must be the effect of a badly timed, rapid conversation, and not a sound clinical intervention. In events of this nature, studies need to investigate the effect of a timely crisis intervention that includes several conversations with the patients. Bisson is one of the professionals who are very critical to PD (see Bisson 1997; Bisson and Deahl 1994). When the critic is based on intervention of an insufficient quality, it does not help the cause to have a good research design.

In addition to these studies Hytten and Hasle (1989) did not find any differences in Impact of Event scores between fire-personnel that participated in debriefing and those who did not following a hotel fire, even though the participants in the debriefing viewed it favourable. Again self-selection determined the group composition, something also present in a study by Matthews (1998). She studied a group of 63 health care workers who experienced violence or other trauma in their work at psychiatric institutions. One week after the event she compared 14 workers who wanted and got debriefing with 18 who were offered but refused, all within the same health district.

In addition she used 31 persons who experienced the same kind of events in another health district as a comparison group. She found the lowest stress level in the district where debriefing was available. The group that chose not to be debriefed had the lowest level of post traumatic stress after one week. One may easily think that those who participated in debriefing were the worst off, since, before the intervention, they were significantly more distressed by what had happened than those who chose not to be debriefed. The author correctly points out that those who experienced the event as most stressful sought the most appropriate way of handling the event; to participate in debriefing. The fact that the stress level was lowest in the area where debriefing was available lead the author to the conclusion that debriefing has a part to play following work related trauma. It must be assumed that debriefing first leads to an increase in distress because it activates emotional networks, as when participants write about a traumatic event. Here research shows a temporary increase in distress but a long-term improvement on different health measures (see Smyth 1998 for a summary). The sole measurement after one week in Matthews' study will not uncover such effects. The study has other obvious limitations, such as self-selection, and shows the complexity of conducting research in this area.

In conclusion, it seems that studies which report no effect of debriefing (or a negative effect; see Bisson *et al.* 1997) have several methodological weaknesses: a) they analyse interventions that only to a limited degree can be called psychological debriefing, b) several studies use self-selection to intervention group and control group, c) it is not clearly defined what the debrief consisted of, d) the timing of the intervention is variable and partly outside the time period recommended for PD, e) the intervention used seems to be clinically insufficient regarding the traumatic event experienced, f) the background and training of the persons who have carried out the interventions is unclear or possibly inadequate, g) the groups in the studies are not comparable, and h) debriefing is investigated in isolation, and not as part of an integrated chain of assistance (CISM).

Particularly the self-selection is a problem in these studies, because it must be presumed that persons who are characterised by avoidance and repression will avoid meetings where they are expected to talk about the event. First of all those who do not feel the need for debriefing because they were peripheral to the event or felt that the event was of little consequence to them will be part of the control group. Secondly, people who use avoidance and denial as a coping strategy will tend to stay away from such meetings. If this 'control' group is compared with a group that through debriefing meetings are encouraged to and 'learn' to put their thoughts and reactions into words, then one would expect the debriefed group to score higher on self-reported reactions (normally being studied).

Additional studies of debriefing

A number of studies have concluded that PD or CISD is followed by a positive effect for the participants (Bohl 1991; Ford *et al.* 1993; Jenkins 1996; Robinson and Mitchell 1993; Stallard and Law 1993; Yule and Udwin 1991). Everly, Flannery and Mitchell (1998) have in addition revised a number of published and unpublished reports and case studies showing positive effects of debriefing. In almost all of the reports (also the negative studies previously described) the participants of the debriefing groups (or individual meetings) when asked to rate their satisfaction or helpfulness experience the meetings as being helpful.

Everly, Boyle and Lating (1998) conducted a meta-analysis based on debriefing studies found in medical and psychological databases. They identified 14 empirical investigations of which 10 were utilised for the analysis. Three were excluded as they failed to use group debriefing interventions and one as it failed to yield data that meaningfully could be used in the analysis. They found a significantly positive effect size (mean Cohen's d = .54, p< .01) resulting from the CISD intervention. The authors comment that this beneficial effect was revealed despite the wide variety of subject groups, the wide range of traumatic events, and the diversity of outcome measures.

However, many of the methodological objections raised in relation to the critical studies also goes for the studies where participants report positive results. A number of very different interventions are being called debriefing, and the extent and the timing of these interventions vary. In addition the training and background of the debriefers are variable, and a lack of control group or self-selection procedure to intervention and control group has taken place. Instead of going through all these studies, a few of the studies will be discussed more thoroughly.

Chemtob et al. (1997) carried out a thorough study regarding 'the influence of debriefing on psychological distress'. In this study they describe how victims of a hurricane had their problems reduced compared to a group who only later received the same type of intervention and who then, after debriefing, report the same reduction in problems. The effectiveness of the intervention was evaluated by the use of the Impact of Event scale used before and following the intervention. There are several objections to this type of design. In addition to lack of data regarding the participants ahead of the debriefing, the participating group was very heterogeneous. Furthermore, the intervention, consisting of PD plus a two hour long lecture on 'post disaster recovery', was carried out six to nine months following the disaster. This study confirmed that PD can be effective a long time after the time period recommended for debriefing, a finding similar to what was reported by Stallard and Law (1993) in their study of adolescents who survived a minibus traffic accident.

Usually PD is practised as one of several interventions following a critical event, often called Critical Incident Stress Management (CISM). Leeman-Conley (1990) documented that an Australian bank introducing CISM following a bank robbery experienced a decline in the number of sick leaves and 'workers' compensation claims' with more than 60 per cent compared with the year ahead of the introduction of the programme, even though the assaults became increasingly more brutal. Flannery and colleagues (reported in Everly, Flannery and Mitchell 1998) report that following the implementation of a CISM programme violence and attacks from patients within a psychiatric setting was reduced with 63 per cent over a two-year period. In addition a reduction in personnel turnover and sick-leaves took place together with a decline in 'workers' compensation claims'. Medical and juridical expenses were also reduced. Because of these results, similar programmes have been started in other places.

In Canada, Western Management Consultants (reported in Everly *et al.* 1998) evaluated a comprehensive CISM programme consisting of among other things preparatory training, individual counselling, and CISD (based on Mitchell) for nurses. Of the persons who participated in a debriefing in this study, 24 per cent reported a decline in personnel turnover, and 99 per cent reported a decline in sick leave days.

The author of this article has not carried out studies on the effect of debriefing. Unpublished data seem to indicate, however, that the participants' perception of the value of PD depends on the amount of experience of the debrief leader (Dyregrov 1996; Kinchin 1998). Where the leader had much experience with the method, almost everyone participating in the debriefing reported that they found the PD useful. In the cases where the leader had less experience, however, a much lower number of participants found the session useful (the majority said that the PD was of some use). Even though the following example has no scientific value, it is still worth mentioning that the person in charge of the follow-up of post office personnel following armed robberies in Bergen, Norway, stated that it was a huge difference between the period before and after PD was routinely installed as part of a CISM programme. Ten years ago, before the psychological follow-up and PD was introduced, a high number of and long sick leaves were common. Today, however, this is no longer a problem.

The many variables affecting the debriefing process and its outcome have been described in more detail elsewhere (Dyregrov 1997). Particularly important is the background of the debriefing leader, and their competence in leading such meetings. With the possibility that debriefing can have a negative effect on the participants (Dyregrov 1997), the group process should be analysed more thoroughly, together with group design, leadership competence, timing, areas of use, individual suitability, etc.

Conclusion

Several studies have been published over the last years concluding that debriefing does not have a positive effect on mental health measures following critical events. These studies are founded on weak methodological designs, and it would be wrong to draw firm conclusions regarding the usefulness of the technique. The majority of the studies have described one single intervention with individual patients, and not the group intervention that PD really is intended to be.

When individuals are receiving help during a crisis, it is not possible to apply the same structure as in PD, without adjusting the process. The group cannot be used in order to normalise reactions, and it cannot be a source of help for the individual members of the group (see Dyregrov 1997, for a description of this group support). Intervention with individuals assumes a different procedure, where the same areas being covered in PD are being processed (facts, thoughts, impressions and reactions). However, the normalisation of reactions depend on the therapist's experience, and there is more freedom to go back and forth between 'phases' talking about the facts, thoughts, impressions and reactions related to the event. This usually demands longer individual follow-up sessions than what has been reported in the studies described herein.

In my opinion the debate on debriefing is not only a scientific but also a political debate. It entails power and positions in the therapeutic world. As a technique presented by Jeffrey T. Mitchell in 1983, PD represented *a threat to the psychiatric professional elite*. Throughout his teachings Mitchell has argued that the traditional psychiatric way of thinking was not appropriate for the population (emergency personnel) for whom the method was developed for, and that health personnel with a psychiatric background often would need to relearn some of their way of thinking and their work methods in order to become good practitioners of the method. In addition, many of the people being trained in the technique both in Australia and North America were peer support personnel and mental health workers working outside psychiatric institutions.

PD thus has been partly self-help and consumer driven where the recipients of services have had more control than in traditional academic or medical approaches based on a more psychiatric disease model. Mitchell has also strongly emphasised that debriefing is not a form of or substitute for psychotherapy (see Mitchell and Everly 1998, p.211). Using PD or CISD as part of crisis intervention has thus been part of a non-psychiatric approach, and therefore it was only natural that there would be a reaction from the 'psychiatric establishment'. The critique in Australia was raised by some of the best known psychiatrists within the trauma field, but it was based on studies that either lacked the methodological quality necessary to support the critique, or studies that investigated the effect of individual follow-up. This, in my point of view, indicates that the debate not only entailed the question of whether debriefing worked or not, but also a more political stance.

Participants of PD report in most cases that they find the groups helpful. Depending on what the group goals are, the groups will be regarded as more or less successful. It is obvious that the groups have a symbolic function, for instance where a group of colleagues or friends have experienced a critical event. Moreover, the group can become a sign that the employer or community cares. So far no good documentation of the preventive effect regarding Post Traumatic Stress Disorder has been produced. However, several studies indicate a marked reduction in costs due to reduction in sick leaves. It must be presumed that PD on its own, without being followed by support and care from leaders and colleagues, or without the possibility for individual follow-up when necessary only has more limited value. PD should be practised in a caring environment and as part of a strategy where the building of a social fellowship within the company or in the local community is central.

One of the positive outcomes of the debate regarding debriefing is the highlighting of several factors that we do not have sufficient knowledge of. Future studies will presumably improve the quality control of psychological debriefing.

Acknowledgements

This article was previously published in *Traumatology: The International Electronic Journal of Innovations in the Study of the Traumatization Process and Methods for Reducing or Eliminating Related Human Suffering* (Autumn, 1998).

References

Avery, A. and Orner, A.A. (1998) 'First report of psychological debriefing abandoned – the end of an era?' *Traumatic Stress Points 12*, 3–4.

Bisson, J.I. (1997) 'Is post-traumatic stress disorder preventable?' *Journal of Mental Health 6*, 109–111.

Bisson, J.I. and Deahl, M.P. (1994) 'Psychological debriefing and prevention of post-traumatic stress.' *British Journal of Psychiatry 165*, 717–720.

Bisson, J.I., Jenkins, P.L., Alexander, J. and Bannister, C. (1997) 'Randomized controlled trial of psychological debriefing for victims of acute burn trauma.' *British Journal of Psychiatry 171*, 78–81.

Bohl, N. (1991) 'The Effectiveness of Brief Psychological Interventions in Police Officers after Critical Incidents.' In J. Reese, J. Horn and C. Dunning (eds) *Critical Incidents in Policing. Revised* (pp.31–38). Washington, DC: U.S. Government Printing Office.

Breslau, N., Davis, G.C., Andreski, P., Peterson, E.L. and Schultz, L.R. (1997) 'Sex differences in posttraumatic stress disorder.' *Archives of General Psychiatry 54*, 1044–1048.

Chemtob, C.M., Tomas, S., Law, W. and Cremniter, D. (1997) 'Postdisaster psychosocial intervention: A field study of the impact of debriefing on psychological distress.' *American Journal of Psychiatry 154*, 415–417.

Deahl, M., Gillham, A.B., Thomas, J., Searle, M.M. and Srinivasan, M. (1994) 'Psychological sequelae following the Gulf war. Factors associated with subsequent morbidity and the effectiveness of psychological debriefing.' *British Journal of Psychiatry 165*, 60–65.

Dyregrov, A. (1989a) 'Caring for helpers in disaster situations: Psychological debriefing.' *Disaster Management 2*, 25–30.

Dyregrov, A. (1989b) 'Retningslinjer for hjelp til familier etter barns død.' *Tidsskrift for Den norske laegeforening 109*, 3408–3411.

Dyregrov, A. (1990) 'Crisis intervention following the loss of an infant child.' *Bereavement Care 9*, 32–35.

Dyregrov, A. (1996) 'The process in critical incident stress debriefings.' Paper presented at the European Conference on Traumatic Stress in Emergency Services Peacekeeping Operations and Humanitarian Aid Organizations. University of Sheffield, UK, 17–20 March.

Dyregrov, A. (1997) 'The process in critical incident stress debriefings.' *Journal of Traumatic Stress 10*, 589–605.

Dyregrov, A. (1998) 'Psychological Debriefing – An Effective Method?' *Traumatology 4*, 2, available at www.fsu.edu/~trauma/art1v4i2.html.

Everly, G.S., Boyle, S.H. and Lating, J.M. (1998) 'Psychological debriefing: A meta-analysis.' Paper presented at the First Nation's Emergency Services Society Critical Incident Stress Conference, 10–14 May, Vancouver, British Columbia, Canada.

Everly, G.S., Flannery, R.B. and Mitchell, J.T. (1998) 'Critical Incident Stress Management (CISM): A review of the literature.' Manuscript submitted for publication.

Ford, J.D., Shaw, D., Sennhauser, S., Greaves, D., Thacker, B., Chandler, P., Schwartz, L. and McClain, V. (1993) 'Psychosocial debriefing after operation desert storm: marital and family assessment and intervention.' *Journal of Social Issues 49*, 73–102.

Hobbs, M., Mayou, R., Harrison, B. and Worlock, P. (1996) 'A randomised controlled trial of psychological debriefing for victims of road traffic accidents.' *British Medical Journal 313*, 1438–1439.

Hytten, K. and Hasle, A. (1989) 'Fire fighters: A study of stress and coping.' *Acta Psychiatrica Scandinavica 80*, Supplementum, 50–55.

Jenkins, S.R. (1996) 'Social support and debriefing efficacy among emergency medical workers after a mass shooting incident.' *Journal of Social Behavior and Personality 11*, 477–492.

Kenardy, J.A., Webster, R.A., Lewing, T.J., Carr, V.J., Hazell, P.L. and Carter, G.L. (1996) 'Stress debriefing and patterns of recovery following a natural disaster.' *Journal of Traumatic Stress 9*, 1, 37–49.

Kinchin, D. (1998) *Post Traumatic Stress Disorder: The Invisible Injury.* Oxon: Success Unlimited.

Kraus, R.P. (1997) 'Psychological debriefing for victims of acute burn trauma (letter to the editor).' *British Journal of Psychiatry 171*, 583.

Lee, C., Slade, P. and Lygo, V. (1996) 'The influence of psychological debriefing on emotional adaptation in women following early miscarriage: a preliminary study.' *British Journal of Medical Psychology 69*, 47–58.

Leeman-Conley, M.M. (1990) 'After a violent robbery…' *Criminology Australia*, April/May, 4–6.

Matthews, L.R. (1998) 'Effect of staff debriefing on post-traumatic stress symptoms after assaults by community housing residents.' *Psychiatric Services 49*, 207–212.

Mitchell, J.T. (1983) 'When disaster strikes… The Critical Incident Stress Debriefing.' *Journal of Emergency Medical Services 8*, 36–39.

Raphael, B., Meldrum, L. and McFarlane, A.C. (1995) 'Does debriefing after psychological trauma work?' *British Medical Journal 310*, 1479–1481.

Robinson, R.C. and Mitchell, J.T. (1993) 'Evaluations of psychological debriefings.' *Journal of Traumatic Stress 6*, 367–382.

Smyth, J.M. (1998) 'Written emotional expression: Effect sizes, outcome types, and moderating variables.' *Journal of Consulting and Clinical Psychology 66*, 174–184.

Stallard, P. and Law, F. (1993) 'Screening and psychological debriefing of adolescent survivors of life-threatening events.' *British Journal of Psychiatry 163*, 660–665.

Turnbull, G., Busuttil, W. and Pittman, S. (1997) 'Psychological debriefing for victims of acute burn trauma (letter to the editor).' *British Journal of Psychiatry 171*, 582.

Yule, W. and Udwin, O. (1991) 'Screening child survivors for post-traumatic stress disorders: Experiences from the *Jupiter* sinking.' *British Journal of Clinical Psychology 30*, 131–138.

Emotional Decompression Prompt Cards

The following set of seven cards, to be used as prompts for Emotional Decompression sessions, are set out here in larger print so that they may be copied and used to aid debriefers who are undertaking a psychological debriefing session.

Introduction

No telephones, disturbances, outsiders

Introduce self: confidentiality clauses

No notes to be taken – except a register

Don't share this with others (except perhaps partners)

'May feel a little worse immediately after the debriefing but this is normal and will soon pass.'

Copyright © David Kinchin 2007

Aim:

To clarify the event and make sense of what you recall. To share your recollections with others. To feel more comfortable with what you may have witnessed.

Facts

Expectations immediately prior to the event

Before... During... Immediately after...

What did you think would happen?

What actually did happen?

How prepared were you? What could have happened?

Feelings

First thoughts: sensory impressions (smells are very important) before, during, after

Emotional reactions. After, just how did you feel?

How do you feel now?

(Watch out for individuals within the group who appear to have difficulties)

Individual vulnerability in situations, feelings afterwards, at home, later that night, right now!

Normalising

These feelings are actually normal (elaborate)

Enforce the 'normal' in all of this

Coping mechanisms

Not everyone will react in the same way

Intrusive images will diminish over time

Don't actually need to react to be normal but it is very normal to react

Future

Local support networks

Sharing emotions and feelings

Important that others understand the impact on YOU

Warning of other events ahead:
          COURT
          FUNERALS
Teaching on PTSD
        (including the snakes and ladders model)

Disengagement

Allow time for questions

Make sure there are sufficient drinks and biscuits!

Give information on self-referral and PTSD and other useful information

Thank people for attending

Make sure YOU stay behind and are able to meet individual needs.

Rebekah – A Psychological Debriefing Session

Rebekah came to me on 9 January 2006, six months and two days after the events and wished to be counselled/debriefed about her experience of them. Rebekah presented as a very normal young woman of bubbly personality. She is well educated and has a very successful career. We both agreed that she could be classified as a 'bit of a political animal'. She has read much about post-traumatic stress and expressed concerns that she might be suffering from the disorder.

She stated clearly that she was not currently taking any medication or receiving any other treatment. She had not suffered a flashback for many months.

Initially, I explored the facts of the events as Rebekah remembered them.

We then continued to explore Rebekah's feelings before, during and after the event.

We concluded with a look at the future, immediate and long term. Immediately after the events, Rebekah was caught up in the memorial services for those who had lost their lives, and it was during the recounting of one of these that she first became very thoughtful and reflective about her situation. She has been particularly struck by the plight of one other woman who had lost her young son during the attacks. Rebekah became very aware that this woman had lost her child, but Rebekah still had her two children to go home to every night.

As her debriefer, I was struck by these aspects of Rebekah's story:

- She was frustrated by the inability of the police service to help her with such mundane tasks as providing her with a crime reference number for the attack.

- She was almost equally frustrated by the way the media stalked her and regularly petitioned her for comments and stories in order to fill news reports and magazine pages.

- Linked more directly, Rebekah was slightly puzzled by the antics and the dialogue she exchanged with the person she perceived to be the bus driver. She wasn't comfortable with the way he said 'it's all over now, you can go' and almost felt there was something sinister in his remarks, as if he knew more than he should about the attacks. This we discussed in detail.

- Finally, she was struck by this woman she observed at the memorial service. At one point, she became convinced that the woman was staring directly at her in a hostile manner.

We undertook some extra work on these four issues and towards the end of our 95-minute session Rebekah appeared to be more at ease with her feelings on all of them. I felt that her interaction with the 'bus-driver' and her feelings towards the grieving mother at the memorial service were the two issues which warranted particular attention.

There is no doubt that Rebekah experienced a very traumatic event, and that she also experienced a traumatic reaction to that event (characterised by at least one flashback to the scene of the immediate aftermath), but she gave me no cause for concern that she had developed full blown Post-Traumatic Stress Disorder (PTSD). I did explain that, although she had not developed the disorder thus far, it was possible that a future event (unknown at present) could act as a trigger and might then start a series of reactions which could be classified as PTSD. However, the more time that passed the less likely this became.

These notes were prepared within 15 hours of our meeting and are a true reflection of what took place, to the best of my recollection.

David Kinchin JP, BEd, CertCPC

Subject Index

Author Index

Alexander, D. 19
American Psychiatric Association 15, 17,
Armstrong, K. 56
Austin, T. 31
Aveline, M. 83

Baugh, J.W. 33
Bohl, N. 53–54
Brewin, C.R. 59–60, 79
British Psychological Association 22

Campbell, J. 83
Cohen, D. 29

Dyrogrov, A. 48, 50, 58, 78, 113–126

Elton, B. 30
Erikson, K.T. 32, 33
Elklit, A. 83

Finer, J. 30

Gleser, G.C. 29
Grace, M.C. 29
Green, B.L. 29

Hanneman, M. 84
Herman, J.I. 22
Hertzer, J. 18
Horowitz, M.J. 94–5, 103
Hough, M. 72

James, L. 29, 32
Johnson, A. 83
Jones, E. 29

Kapp, F.T. 29
Kinchin, D. 48, 52, 75, 95–9, 127–130,
    131–2
Kirchenbaum, H. 83
Korol, M. 29

Lacey, G. 31
Leonard, A.C. 29

Mayou, R. 39
McNally, V. 54–5
Miller, J. 31
Mitchell, J. 48–9, 56, 74, 88, 90
Moran, W.C. 27

Owen, Mr Justice 26

Parkinson, F. 28, 47–8, 51, 68, 80, 91

Quinton, A. 102–3

Raphael, B. 54, 60
Regehr, C. 55–6

Saari, S. 83
Saylor, L. 29
Stern, G.M. 29